Pacific Coast Highway
Road Trip Guide

From Vancouver, B.C. to San Diego, CA

by Brian Eagen

WHEN TO VISIT

The entire length of the pacific coast can be driven any time of the year, but weather, crowds, and wildlife migratory routes each have their prime times. Here's a little insight to help you decide when YOU would like to explore each area.

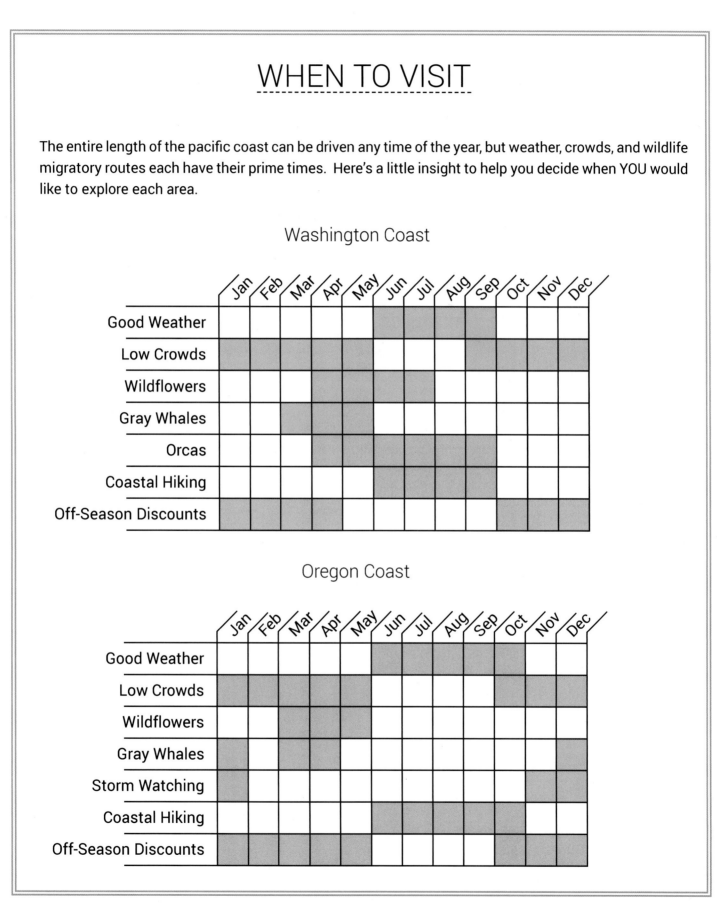

Washington Coast

	Jan	Feb	Mar	Apr	May	Jun	Jul	Aug	Sep	Oct	Nov	Dec
Good Weather						■	■	■	■			
Low Crowds	■	■	■	■	■				■	■	■	■
Wildflowers				■	■	■	■					
Gray Whales			■	■	■							
Orcas				■	■	■	■	■	■			
Coastal Hiking						■	■	■	■			
Off-Season Discounts	■	■	■	■						■	■	■

Oregon Coast

	Jan	Feb	Mar	Apr	May	Jun	Jul	Aug	Sep	Oct	Nov	Dec
Good Weather						■	■	■	■	■		
Low Crowds	■	■	■	■	■					■	■	■
Wildflowers			■	■	■							
Gray Whales	■		■	■								■
Storm Watching	■										■	■
Coastal Hiking						■	■	■	■	■		
Off-Season Discounts	■	■	■	■	■					■	■	■

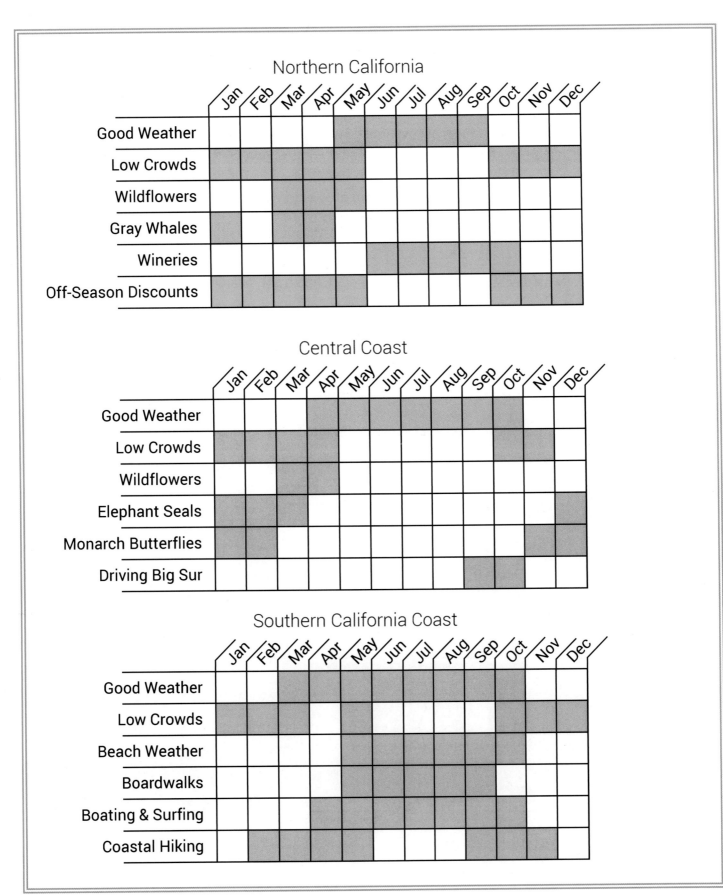

BUDGETING

Budgeting for a road trip is one of the most overlooked tools for a successful and stress-free adventure. Costs for your trip can be broken down into four main categories; *gas*, *food*, *lodging*, and *permit fees*.

Gas is estimated by taking the total mileage (plus a little extra to be safe), dividing by your vehicle's miles-per-gallon, and multiplying by the current fuel costs.

We estimate **food costs** by taking the number of people times the number of days of the trip, and multiplying that by a daily food cost ($8 is an average amount, and a good place to start).

Lodging (or camping) is calculated by nightly fees times number of nights.

Permit fees include miscellaneous costs such as entrance fees, guide fees, trail permits, or other services.

Fill in the blanks below to quickly create an accurate budget for your upcoming trip.

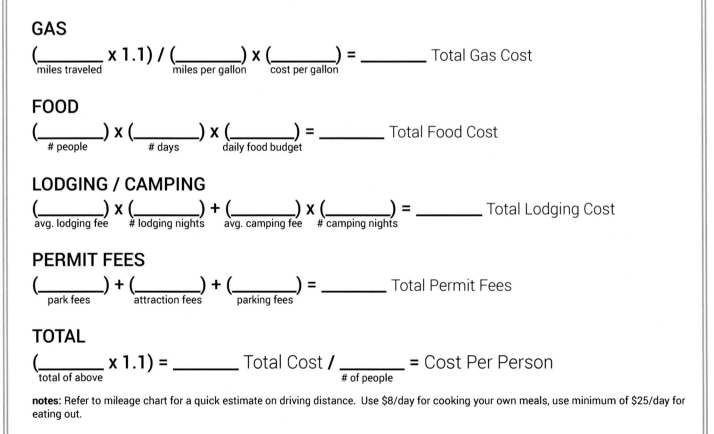

GAS
(_____ x 1.1) / (_____) x (_____) = _____ Total Gas Cost
 miles traveled   miles per gallon   cost per gallon

FOOD
(_____) x (_____) x (_____) = _____ Total Food Cost
  # people   # days   daily food budget

LODGING / CAMPING
(_____) x (_____) + (_____) x (_____) = _____ Total Lodging Cost
 avg. lodging fee   # lodging nights   avg. camping fee   # camping nights

PERMIT FEES
(_____) + (_____) + (_____) = _____ Total Permit Fees
   park fees   attraction fees   parking fees

TOTAL
(_____ x 1.1) = _____ Total Cost / _____ = Cost Per Person
 total of above   # of people

notes: Refer to mileage chart for a quick estimate on driving distance. Use $8/day for cooking your own meals, use minimum of $25/day for eating out.

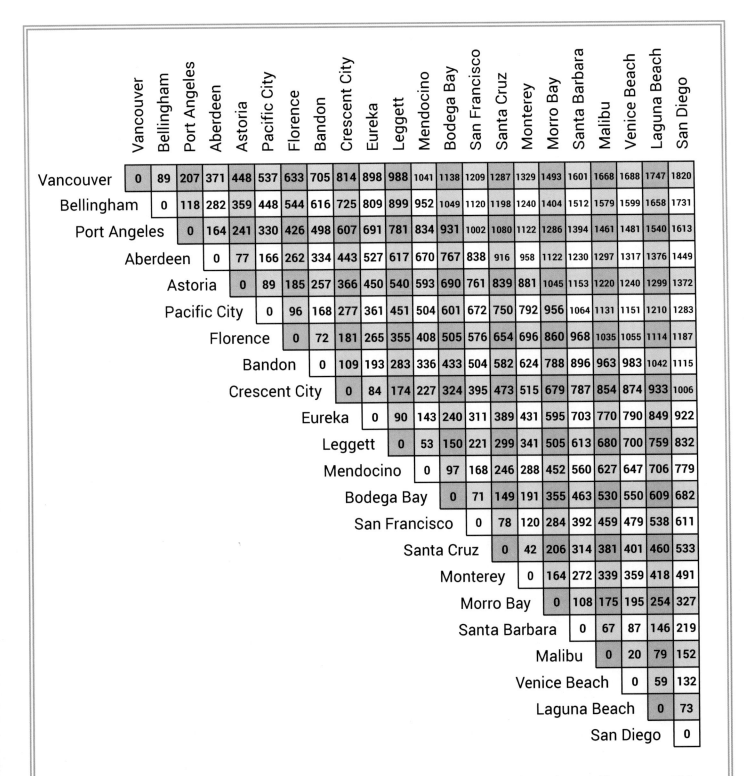

	Vancouver	Bellingham	Port Angeles	Aberdeen	Astoria	Pacific City	Florence	Bandon	Crescent City	Eureka	Leggett	Mendocino	Bodega Bay	San Francisco	Santa Cruz	Monterey	Morro Bay	Santa Barbara	Malibu	Venice Beach	Laguna Beach	San Diego
Vancouver	0	89	207	371	448	537	633	705	814	898	988	1041	1138	1209	1287	1329	1493	1601	1668	1688	1747	1820
Bellingham		0	118	282	359	448	544	616	725	809	899	952	1049	1120	1198	1240	1404	1512	1579	1599	1658	1731
Port Angeles			0	164	241	330	426	498	607	691	781	834	931	1002	1080	1122	1286	1394	1461	1481	1540	1613
Aberdeen				0	77	166	262	334	443	527	617	670	767	838	916	958	1122	1230	1297	1317	1376	1449
Astoria					0	89	185	257	366	450	540	593	690	761	839	881	1045	1153	1220	1240	1299	1372
Pacific City						0	96	168	277	361	451	504	601	672	750	792	956	1064	1131	1151	1210	1283
Florence							0	72	181	265	355	408	505	576	654	696	860	968	1035	1055	1114	1187
Bandon								0	109	193	283	336	433	504	582	624	788	896	963	983	1042	1115
Crescent City									0	84	174	227	324	395	473	515	679	787	854	874	933	1006
Eureka										0	90	143	240	311	389	431	595	703	770	790	849	922
Leggett											0	53	150	221	299	341	505	613	680	700	759	832
Mendocino												0	97	168	246	288	452	560	627	647	706	779
Bodega Bay													0	71	149	191	355	463	530	550	609	682
San Francisco														0	78	120	284	392	459	479	538	611
Santa Cruz															0	42	206	314	381	401	460	533
Monterey																0	164	272	339	359	418	491
Morro Bay																	0	108	175	195	254	327
Santa Barbara																		0	67	87	146	219
Malibu																			0	20	79	152
Venice Beach																				0	59	132
Laguna Beach																					0	73
San Diego																						0

You could spend a lifetime exploring all of the hikes, towns, and sights along the pacific coast. This guide is just the tip of the iceberg when it comes to all of the amazing things you can do. So get going! And be sure to **tag your photos** with **#OutsideYourself** to share your journey with the Outdoor Blueprint community along the way.

DAY 1   date _____   start _____   end _____   drive time _____

TODAY'S ACTIVITIES

1)

2)

3)

breakfast at: ....

lunch at: ....

dinner at: ....

drinks at: ....

additional notes

DAY 2   date _____   start _____   end _____   drive time _____

TODAY'S ACTIVITIES

1)

2)

3)

breakfast at: ....

lunch at: ....

dinner at: ....

drinks at: ....

additional notes

DAY 3   date _____   start _____   end _____   drive time _____

TODAY'S ACTIVITIES

1)

2)

3)

breakfast at: ....

lunch at: ....

dinner at: ....

drinks at: ....

additional notes

DAY 4   date _____   start _____   end _____   drive time _____

TODAY'S ACTIVITIES

1)

2)

3)

breakfast at: ....

lunch at: ....

dinner at: ....

drinks at: ....

additional notes

DAY 5

date _____ start _____ end _____ drive time _____

TODAY'S ACTIVITIES

1)

2)

3)

breakfast at: ....
lunch at: ....
dinner at: ....
drinks at: ....

additional notes

DAY 6

date _____ start _____ end _____ drive time _____

TODAY'S ACTIVITIES

1)

2)

3)

breakfast at: ....
lunch at: ....
dinner at: ....
drinks at: ....

additional notes

DAY 7

date _____ start _____ end _____ drive time _____

TODAY'S ACTIVITIES

1)

2)

3)

breakfast at: ....
lunch at: ....
dinner at: ....
drinks at: ....

additional notes

DAY 8

date _____ start _____ end _____ drive time _____

TODAY'S ACTIVITIES

1)

2)

3)

breakfast at: ....
lunch at: ....
dinner at: ....
drinks at: ....

additional notes

PACKING LIST

VEHICLE
- The PCH Road Trip Guide
- Atlas or State Maps
- Jumper Cables
- A Recent Tune-Up
- Small Blanket
- USB Charging Port

PERSONAL
- Sun Hat, Sunscreen, Lip Balm
- Sunglasses
- Warm Hat
- Shirts
- Rain Jacket
- Puffy Coat, Fleece, or other Warm Jacket
- Underwear
- Short / Pants
- Socks
- Hiking Shoes
- Beach / Camp Shoes
- City Shoes
- Swimming Suit
- Toiletries
- Phone + Charging Cords
- Water Bottle
- Book, Journal, Pen

CAMPING
- Tent
- Sleeping Bag (per person)
- Sleeping Pad (per person)
- Headlamp (per person)
- Pillow (per person)
- Camp Chair (per person)

COOKING
- Stove (a 2-burner propane stove works well)
- Fuel + Lighter
- Cookware (small pot and pan)
- Cooking Utensils (serving spoon, spatula, tongs, can opener, pot grips, knife)
- Small Cutting Board
- Plates and/or Bowls (per person)
- Spoon, Fork, Knife (per person)
- Small Bottle of Biodegradable Dish Soap
- Wash Cloth & Small Dish Towel
- Mug (per person)
- Medium Cooler
- Extra Trash Bags (grocery bags work well)

Organizing is key on long road trips, especially if you're camping along the way. The 10 and 14 gallon Rubbermaid Roughnecks are my go-to storage container -- you can find them at local hardware stores for $10. Here's the system I've developed over countless road trips:

- Small suitcase or bag for personal clothing items
- Separate plastic bag for dirty laundry
- 10 gallon Roughneck for cooking items
- 14 gallon Roughneck for non-perishable food
- Medium-sized cooler for cold food with a tupperware full of ice (you can replenish the ice at gas stations and fast food stops)
- Use large items such as the tent, sleeping bags, and sleeping pads to fill gaps

Use the extra plastic grocery bags for disposing of daily trash and containing messy items like wet shoes.

MUST-HAVE APPS for your ROAD TRIP

Smartphones have changed the road tripping game in so many ways -- navigation, entertainment, and finding nearby attractions, just to name a few. Here's my list of must-have apps that can enrich your road tripping experience and save you money!

iExit - FOR A QUICK AMENITIES OVERVIEW   FREE   Android / iOS

iExit is a great place to start when searching for basic amenities such as food, gas, rest stops, camping, and more. There are a TON of locations packed into this app. You won't find much information about each place, but if you're just trying to make a quick stop and want some gas and food, this app is a great go-to.

Wave - FOR NAVIGATION   FREE   Android / iOS

Turn-by-turn navigation that is constantly updating based on traffic and road conditions. Pre-set common locations such as your home, work, and frequently visited spots for quick navigation. Watch out for traffic jams, police, and road construction with the help of millions of other users.

Hotel Tonight - FOR LODGING ARRANGEMENTS   FREE   Android / iOS

A great way to find last minute deals on great hotels in your area. Search for a hotel, figure out what amenities it has, read some reviews, and book it -- all in a couple of minutes. Finding a spot to sleep at night should be stress-free, and this is one great way to do it.

The Ultimate US Public Campground Project - FOR CAMPING $3.99   Android / iOS

For the most comprehensive campground database, look no further than Ultimate US Public Campground Project. Quickly find a campsite according to: land agency, elevation, cost, amenities, water, and activities. It even includes many dispersed camping areas.

GasBuddy - FOR THE CHEAPEST GAS   FREE   Android / iOS

Always know exactly where the cheapest gas is located and how to get there with GasBuddy. Search for nearby locations or enter a city. Help keep the prices updated to be eligible to win some free gas along the way.

TVfoodMaps - FOR DELICIOUS FOOD   FREE   Android / iOS

For an Anthony Bourdain-style road trip, you cannot beat TVfoodMaps. This app pulls up all of the great restaurants that have been featured on TV shows, plus helpful tips from other travelers who have eaten there.

SitOrSquat - FOR EMERGENCY BATHROOM BREAKS   FREE   Android / iOS

Never have a bathroom emergency again. SitOrSquat quickly maps out all of the nearby restroom locations and allows you to filter based on quality, handicap accessibility, baby changing tables, and whether or not it's free. Then, quickly navigate to your chosen bath room with the directions button.

Audible - FOR ROADSIDE ENTERTAINMENT   In-App Puchases   Android / iOS

Nothing beats listening to an audiobook while busting through some less exciting miles. Audible allows you to play popular books, find new books, and keep tabs on where you are in each book (if you like to jump around).

Snapseed - FOR PHOTOGRAPHY   FREE   Android / iOS

Bring the power of professional photo editing software straight to your mobile device. Snapseed is my go-to method for retouching and embellishing photos. Crop, vignette, tune, and save your images so they are ready to share with the world.

HONK - FOR AUTO MAINTENANCE   Fee based on services   Android / iOS

Get the help you need when your car breaks down with this easy app. Whether it's a flat tire, dead battery, empty gas tank, locked door, or mechanical breakdown - HONK will quickly get someone sent your way. Prices from different companies will be quoted based on vehicle needs and location.

Findery - FOR FINDING NEARBY ATTRACTIONS   FREE   Android / iOS

Findery provides a quick look at what's nearby. From historical spots to famous attractions, this is my go-to app when I'm looking for something interesting to do on the fly. Since this is user-curated, you never know what you're going to get -- but it sure is interesting to take a look.

Bonjournal (journi for Android) - FOR TRIP DOCUMENTATION   FREE   Android / iOS

Document and share all of your adventures with Bonjournal (or journi for Android). These apps create a mini-blog platform complete with pictures and journal entries so you can keep track of each day's activities forever! Both apps are easy to learn, minimal in design, and focus on documenting YOUR adventures.

ParkMe - FOR FINDING PARKING   FREE   Android / iOS

Search for street, lot, and meter parking while filtering by time, payment type, and more. This app is great for when you're visiting cities and want to know where to ditch the car. You can even reserve a spot in certain lots.

Trip Splitter Lite - FOR FINANCIAL TRACKING   FREE   Android / iOS

Keep all of your expenses in order -- even while traveling with a large group! This app tracks who spent how much on what, so that you can even up at the end of the trip (or even along the way). Trip Splitter Lite only allows splitting between two people. Upgrade to the $1.99 version for unlimited splitting. On Android look for Splitomatic, a similar app.

Glympse - FOR LOCATION TRACKING   FREE   Android / iOS

Are you planning on traveling with a group or meeting up with others along the way? Share you location and ETA by sending a Glympse. The app sends a text and allows others to follow along with your progress live, which minimizes waiting around.

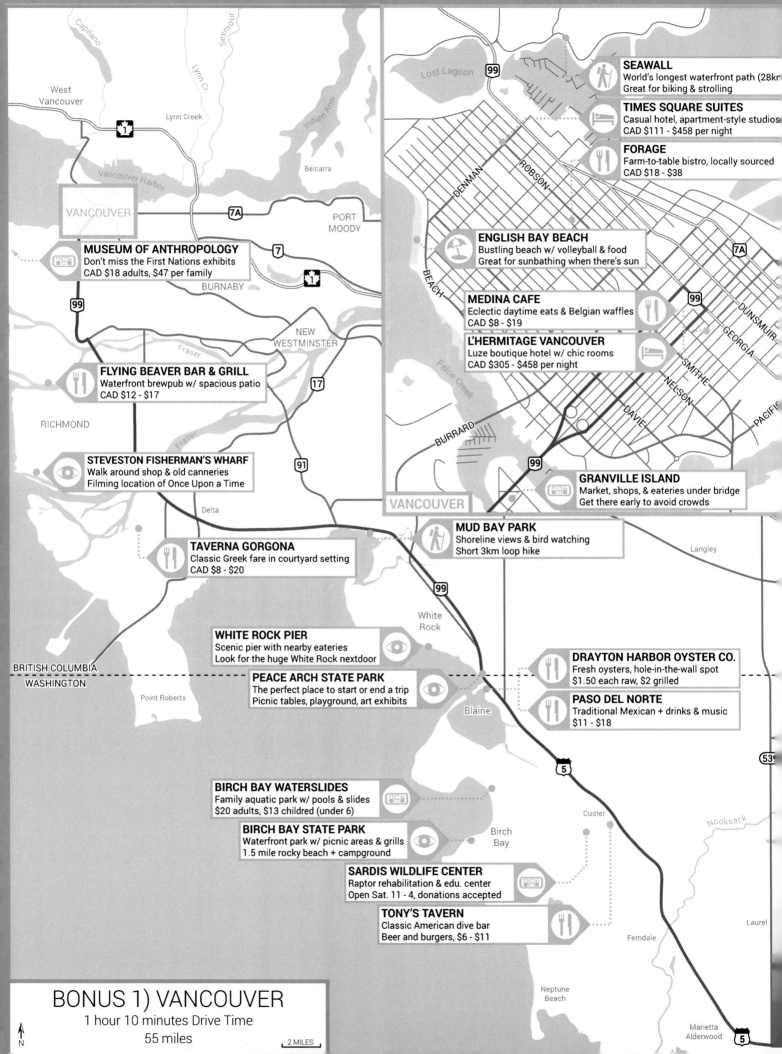

SEAWALL
World's longest waterfront path (28km)
Great for biking & strolling

TIMES SQUARE SUITES
Casual hotel, apartment-style studios
CAD $111 - $458 per night

FORAGE
Farm-to-table bistro, locally sourced
CAD $18 - $38

ENGLISH BAY BEACH
Bustling beach w/ volleyball & food
Great for sunbathing when there's sun

MEDINA CAFE
Eclectic daytime eats & Belgian waffles
CAD $8 - $19

L'HERMITAGE VANCOUVER
Luze boutique hotel w/ chic rooms
CAD $305 - $458 per night

MUSEUM OF ANTHROPOLOGY
Don't miss the First Nations exhibits
CAD $18 adults, $47 per family

FLYING BEAVER BAR & GRILL
Waterfront brewpub w/ spacious patio
CAD $12 - $17

STEVESTON FISHERMAN'S WHARF
Walk around shop & old canneries
Filming location of Once Upon a Time

GRANVILLE ISLAND
Market, shops, & eateries under bridge
Get there early to avoid crowds

MUD BAY PARK
Shoreline views & bird watching
Short 3km loop hike

TAVERNA GORGONA
Classic Greek fare in courtyard setting
CAD $8 - $20

WHITE ROCK PIER
Scenic pier with nearby eateries
Look for the huge White Rock nextdoor

DRAYTON HARBOR OYSTER CO.
Fresh oysters, hole-in-the-wall spot
$1.50 each raw, $2 grilled

PEACE ARCH STATE PARK
The perfect place to start or end a trip
Picnic tables, playground, art exhibits

PASO DEL NORTE
Traditional Mexican + drinks & music
$11 - $18

BIRCH BAY WATERSLIDES
Family aquatic park w/ pools & slides
$20 adults, $13 childred (under 6)

BIRCH BAY STATE PARK
Waterfront park w/ picnic areas & grills
1.5 mile rocky beach + campground

SARDIS WILDLIFE CENTER
Raptor rehabilitation & edu. center
Open Sat. 11 - 4, donations accepted

TONY'S TAVERN
Classic American dive bar
Beer and burgers, $6 - $11

BONUS 1) VANCOUVER
1 hour 10 minutes Drive Time
55 miles

2 MILES

N

VANCOUVER, B.C.

Potlatch: A Ceremony of Giving

One of the cornerstones of culture for the Pacific Northwest First Nations was the potlatch. A potlatch was a ceremony of gift giving to reaffirm social standings. Potlatches were thrown on occasions when a new heir was stepping into power and needed to assert their social position, such as marriages, deaths, and initiations. However, even small events could be the cause for throwing a potlatch, such as when two rivals have suffered public embarrassment.

Material wealth was important to nations of the pacific northwest, so by giving it away they raised their family's status. In some ways a potlatch was similar to taxation, where wealthy families gave away their surplus wealth to the group.

Each nation had their own nuances when it came to the potlatch, but there were some overall themes including; songs, dances, and rituals revolving around the host family's ancestry. The host family would shower his guest with lavish gifts who in turn would validate the passing along of social title. Sometimes chiefs would accumulate wealth over years before hosting a potlatch. Every member of the tribe was responsible for contributing, but only based on their standing within the tribe. The chief was required to contribute the most.

Potlatches continued for days at a time, as guest tribes arrived and were fed two massive meals each day. Gifts, such as Hudson Bay Blankets, canoes, coppers, kettles, and slaves were given according to rank. Upon returning to their town, the chief would frequently redistribute the wealth they received among the entire tribe.

Canadian and United States authorities both saw the potlatch ritual as wasteful and outlawed the process in the late 1800s. For 70 years potlatching discretely continued, but not without numerous individuals being jailed for participating in the practice. Finally, in the 1950s the law was repealed and many nations continue the practice to this day.

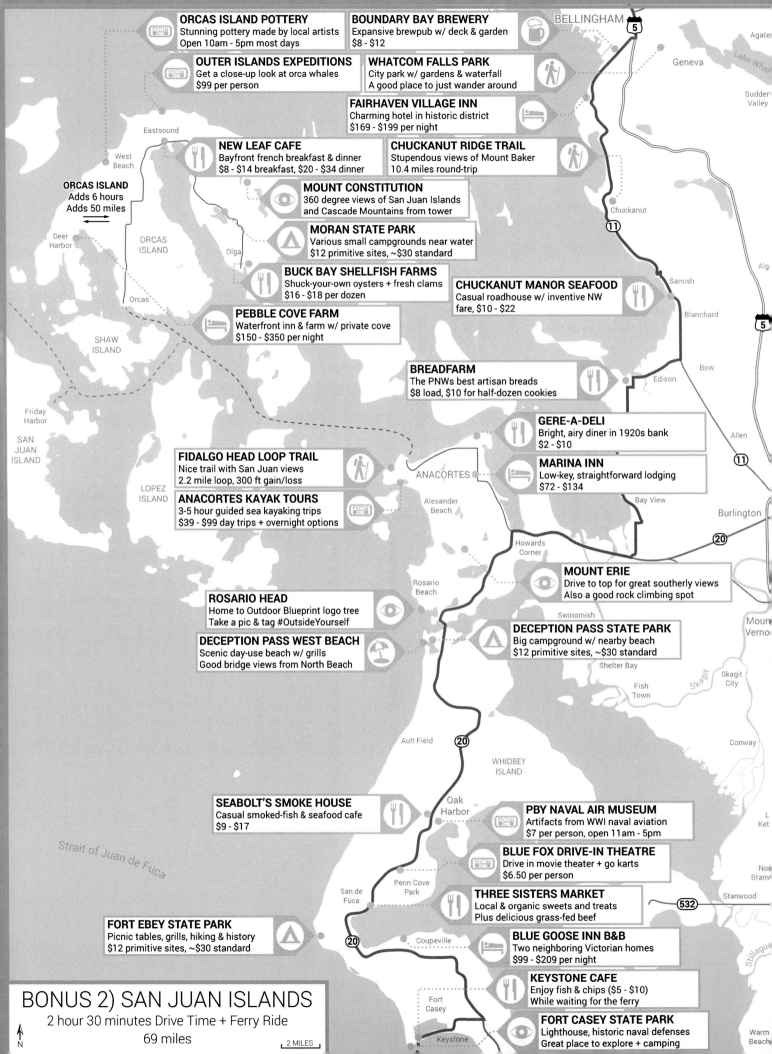

ORCAS ISLAND POTTERY
Stunning pottery made by local artists
Open 10am - 5pm most days

BOUNDARY BAY BREWERY
Expansive brewpub w/ deck & garden
$8 - $12

BELLINGHAM

OUTER ISLANDS EXPEDITIONS
Get a close-up look at orca whales
$99 per person

WHATCOM FALLS PARK
City park w/ gardens & waterfall
A good place to just wander around

FAIRHAVEN VILLAGE INN
Charming hotel in historic district
$169 - $199 per night

Eastsound

NEW LEAF CAFE
Bayfront french breakfast & dinner
$8 - $14 breakfast, $20 - $34 dinner

CHUCKANUT RIDGE TRAIL
Stupendous views of Mount Baker
10.4 miles round-trip

West
Beach

ORCAS ISLAND
Adds 6 hours
Adds 50 miles

MOUNT CONSTITUTION
360 degree views of San Juan Islands
and Cascade Mountains from tower

Chuckanut

Deer
Harbor

ORCAS
ISLAND

Olga

MORAN STATE PARK
Various small campgrounds near water
$12 primitive sites, ~$30 standard

Samish

Orcas

BUCK BAY SHELLFISH FARMS
Shuck-your-own oysters + fresh clams
$16 - $18 per dozen

CHUCKANUT MANOR SEAFOOD
Casual roadhouse w/ inventive NW
fare, $10 - $22

Blanchard

SHAW
ISLAND

PEBBLE COVE FARM
Waterfront inn & farm w/ private cove
$150 - $350 per night

Bow

Friday
Harbor

BREADFARM
The PNWs best artisan breads
$8 load, $10 for half-dozen cookies

Edison

SAN
JUAN
ISLAND

GERE-A-DELI
Bright, airy diner in 1920s bank
$2 - $10

Allen

FIDALGO HEAD LOOP TRAIL
Nice trail with San Juan views
2.2 mile loop, 300 ft gain/loss

ANACORTES

MARINA INN
Low-key, straightforward lodging
$72 - $134

LOPEZ
ISLAND

Alexander
Beach

Bay View

Burlington

ANACORTES KAYAK TOURS
3-5 hour guided sea kayaking trips
$39 - $99 day trips + overnight options

Howards
Corner

MOUNT ERIE
Drive to top for great southerly views
Also a good rock climbing spot

Rosario
Beach

Swinomish

DECEPTION PASS STATE PARK
Big campground w/ nearby beach
$12 primitive sites, ~$30 standard

ROSARIO HEAD
Home to Outdoor Blueprint logo tree
Take a pic & tag #OutsideYourself

Moun
Verno

DECEPTION PASS WEST BEACH
Scenic day-use beach w/ grills
Good bridge views from North Beach

Shelter Bay

Fish
Town

Skagit
City

Ault Field

WHIDBEY
ISLAND

Conway

SEABOLT'S SMOKE HOUSE
Casual smoked-fish & seafood cafe
$9 - $17

Oak
Harbor

PBY NAVAL AIR MUSEUM
Artifacts from WWI naval aviation
$7 per person, open 11am - 5pm

Strait of Juan de Fuca

BLUE FOX DRIVE-IN THEATRE
Drive in movie theater + go karts
$6.50 per person

Penn Cove
Park

THREE SISTERS MARKET
Local & organic sweets and treats
Plus delicious grass-fed beef

Stanwood

San de
Fuca

FORT EBEY STATE PARK
Picnic tables, grills, hiking & history
$12 primitive sites, ~$30 standard

Coupeville

BLUE GOOSE INN B&B
Two neighboring Victorian homes
$99 - $209 per night

BONUS 2) SAN JUAN ISLANDS
2 hour 30 minutes Drive Time + Ferry Ride
69 miles

Fort
Casey

KEYSTONE CAFE
Enjoy fish & chips ($5 - $10)
While waiting for the ferry

Keystone

FORT CASEY STATE PARK
Lighthouse, historic naval defenses
Great place to explore + camping

N

2 MILES

WASHINGTON

The Washington section of Highway 101 is the most remote region along the United States pacific coast. Despite Highway 101's distance from the water, there are some amazing opportunities to adventure and explore. Olympic National Park provides a unique blend of alpine, rain forest, and coastal environments for hikers and sightseers while the small coastal towns of Raymond, Aberdeen, Westport, and Seaside offer delicious food, cute lodging, and fun local museums.

SAN JUAN ISLANDS

Home of Orcas

The San Juan Islands are home to three resident orca families, known as the J, K, and L pods. These three pods, referred to as the Southern Residents, can be found throughout the archipelago from spring to autumn. Each pod represents an extended family group revolving around the oldest female. J pod, comprised of 29 orcas according to the Center for Whale Research, is home to a orca named "Granny" who is estimated to be 103 year old!

There are four communities of orcas along the pacific coast, the Southern Residents (of the San Juan Islands), the Northern Residents (of the British Columbia), the Offshores (found 25 miles offshore from Vancouver Island), and the Transients (small groups from Mexico to the Bering Strait). Each community has its own distinct diet, behavior, and dialect. For instance, the Southern Residents eat primarily salmon, while the Transients eat marine mammals such as seals and porpoises.

If you're interested in getting a closer look, there are a number of motorized and sailboat whale watching companies to choose from. You can find them on each of the four main islands along with the town of Anacortes. Kayak tours are another great way to get out on the water, and it's not uncommon to get a close up view of the orcas along the way. Lime Kiln Point State Park, located on San Juan Islands, is a great spot for shore-based whale watching.

There is an entire collection of museums and attractions, known as "The Whale Trail," located throughout Puget Sound. These educational sites are great ways to educate yourself about orca habitat and behavior. See the full map at *thewhaletrail.org*

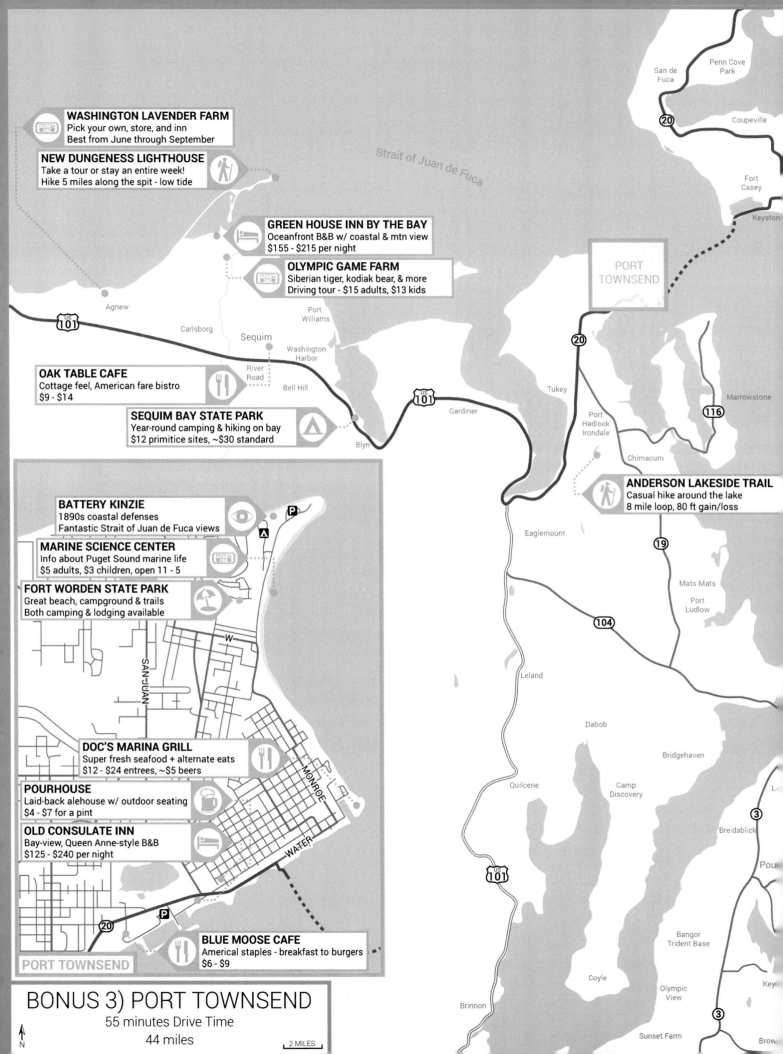

WASHINGTON LAVENDER FARM
Pick your own, store, and inn
Best from June through September

NEW DUNGENESS LIGHTHOUSE
Take a tour or stay an entire week!
Hike 5 miles along the spit - low tide

GREEN HOUSE INN BY THE BAY
Oceanfront B&B w/ coastal & mtn view
$155 - $215 per night

OLYMPIC GAME FARM
Siberian tiger, kodiak bear, & more
Driving tour - $15 adults, $13 kids

OAK TABLE CAFE
Cottage feel, American fare bistro
$9 - $14

SEQUIM BAY STATE PARK
Year-round camping & hiking on bay
$12 primitice sites, ~$30 standard

BATTERY KINZIE
1890s coastal defenses
Fantastic Strait of Juan de Fuca views

MARINE SCIENCE CENTER
Info about Puget Sound marine life
$5 adults, $3 children, open 11 - 5

FORT WORDEN STATE PARK
Great beach, campground & trails
Both camping & lodging available

DOC'S MARINA GRILL
Super fresh seafood + alternate eats
$12 - $24 entrees, ~$5 beers

POURHOUSE
Laid-back alehouse w/ outdoor seating
$4 - $7 for a pint

OLD CONSULATE INN
Bay-view, Queen Anne-style B&B
$125 - $240 per night

BLUE MOOSE CAFE
Americal staples - breakfast to burgers
$6 - $9

ANDERSON LAKESIDE TRAIL
Casual hike around the lake
8 mile loop, 80 ft gain/loss

BONUS 3) PORT TOWNSEND
55 minutes Drive Time
44 miles

2 MILES

PORT TOWNSEND

Olympic Coast National Marine Sanctuary: Local advice from Discovery Center

Olympic Coast National Marine Sanctuary represents one of North America's most productive marine ecosystems and wilderness shorelines. Significant natural and cultural resources include 29 species of marine mammals, large populations of nesting seabirds, shipwrecks, and some of the most spectacular wilderness coastline in the lower 48 states.

The wild character of Olympic Coast makes it a unique destination. The ocean shore provides endless opportunities for discovery and investigation. Hiking, backpacking and camping are popular in the coastal wilderness strip of Olympic National Park.

Respectful exploration of intertidal sea life fascinates beachgoers. Tidepooling is exciting for all ages. When the sea recedes, it reveals a world that is both on-land and underwater for part of every day. Up-close encounters with intertidal animals require being respectful. The sanctuary's tidepool etiquette webpage provides tips on minimizing impact.

Wildlife watching is superb. Birding and whale watching are very rewarding throughout the year along the coast.

Diving in Olympic Coast National Marine Sanctuary is popular among expert divers. Exceptional habitats, fish populations go hand in hand with the coast's extreme conditions. A few dive charter operators serve the Olympic Coast - in general, ocean conditions and isolation require advanced skills and exposed open-water experience.

The Olympic Coast provides challenge for expert sea kayakers. Extreme conditions (and extremely changeable conditions) make this environment truly exceptional. Locals and a growing number of surfers from Seattle and beyond have discovered the challenges and rewards of Olympic Coast breaks, fueled by big Pacific swells.

Sport-fishing charters for salmon, halibut, ling cod and occasionally, albacore tuna, are available from Neah Bay, Sekiu, La Push and Westport. Fall, winter and spring low tides are popular for razor clamming. Fishing and shellfish gathering are regulated and licenses are required.

All coastal visitors should monitor conditions before departing, knowing weather, tides and currents and, above all, exercising caution in this extreme and remote environment.

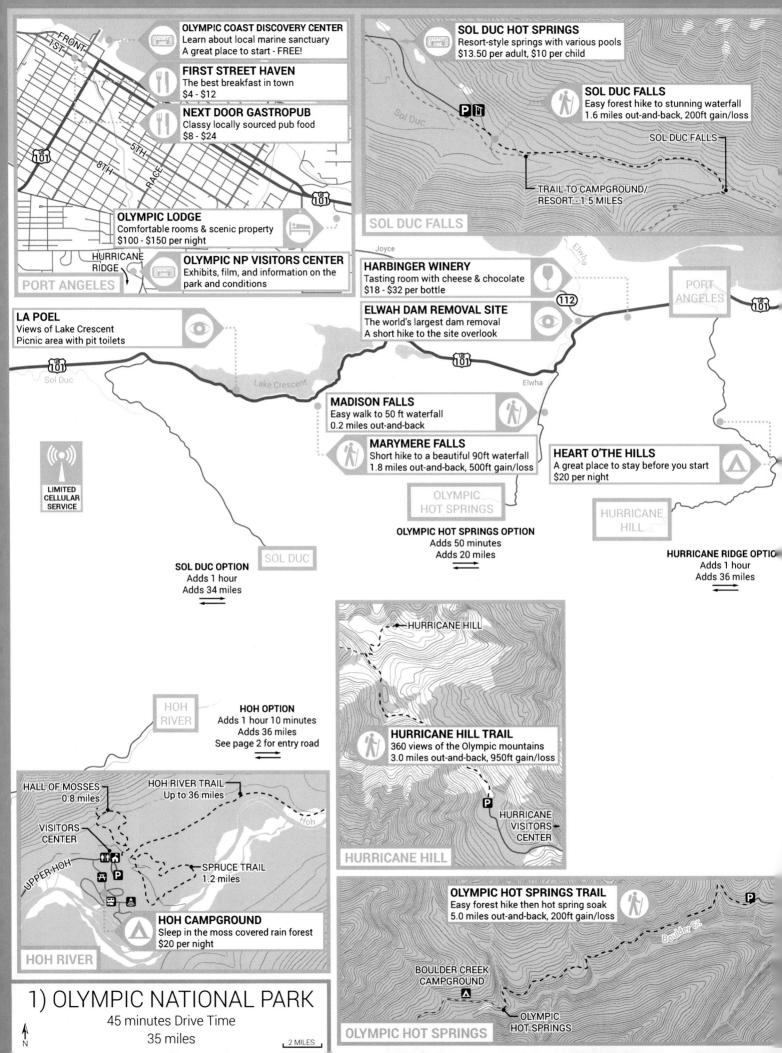

OLYMPIC COAST DISCOVERY CENTER
Learn about local marine sanctuary
A great place to start - FREE!

FIRST STREET HAVEN
The best breakfast in town
$4 - $12

NEXT DOOR GASTROPUB
Classy locally sourced pub food
$8 - $24

OLYMPIC LODGE
Comfortable rooms & scenic property
$100 - $150 per night

OLYMPIC NP VISITORS CENTER
Exhibits, film, and information on the
park and conditions

PORT ANGELES

HURRICANE RIDGE

LA POEL
Views of Lake Crescent
Picnic area with pit toilets

Lake Crescent

Sol Duc

LIMITED CELLULAR SERVICE

SOL DUC HOT SPRINGS
Resort-style springs with various pools
$13.50 per adult, $10 per child

SOL DUC FALLS
Easy forest hike to stunning waterfall
1.6 miles out-and-back, 200ft gain/loss

SOL DUC FALLS

TRAIL TO CAMPGROUND/
RESORT - 1.5 MILES

SOL DUC FALLS

Joyce

HARBINGER WINERY
Tasting room with cheese & chocolate
$18 - $32 per bottle

ELWAH DAM REMOVAL SITE
The world's largest dam removal
A short hike to the site overlook

Elwha

PORT ANGELES

MADISON FALLS
Easy walk to 50 ft waterfall
0.2 miles out-and-back

MARYMERE FALLS
Short hike to a beautiful 90ft waterfall
1.8 miles out-and-back, 500ft gain/loss

HEART O'THE HILLS
A great place to stay before you start
$20 per night

OLYMPIC
HOT SPRINGS

HURRICANE
HILL

OLYMPIC HOT SPRINGS OPTION
Adds 50 minutes
Adds 20 miles

HURRICANE RIDGE OPTION
Adds 1 hour
Adds 36 miles

SOL DUC OPTION
Adds 1 hour
Adds 34 miles

SOL DUC

HOH OPTION
Adds 1 hour 10 minutes
Adds 36 miles
See page 2 for entry road

HOH
RIVER

HURRICANE HILL

HURRICANE HILL TRAIL
360 views of the Olympic mountains
3.0 miles out-and-back, 950ft gain/loss

HURRICANE
VISITORS
CENTER

HURRICANE HILL

HALL OF MOSSES
0.8 miles

HOH RIVER TRAIL
Up to 36 miles

VISITORS
CENTER

UPPER HOH

Hoh

SPRUCE TRAIL
1.2 miles

HOH CAMPGROUND
Sleep in the moss covered rain forest
$20 per night

HOH RIVER

OLYMPIC HOT SPRINGS TRAIL
Easy forest hike then hot spring soak
5.0 miles out-and-back, 200ft gain/loss

Boulder Ct

BOULDER CREEK
CAMPGROUND

OLYMPIC
HOT SPRINGS

OLYMPIC HOT SPRINGS

1) OLYMPIC NATIONAL PARK
45 minutes Drive Time
35 miles

N

2 MILES

OLYMPIC NATIONAL PARK

A Brief History of Port Angeles

Port Angeles is situated at the northernmost point of Highway 101, which makes it a logical starting point for the Pacific Coast Highway road trip guide. Highway 101 actually continues around the entire Olympic Peninsula, heading down the western side of Puget Sound, and eventual terminating just outside of Olympia, Washington. Port Angeles has a long history of settlement, from native tribes to Spanish explorers and finally European Americans. All of the towns in this area, including Port Angeles, were slow to grow due to their remote location. It wasn't until the development of a full scale trading post that the town began to develop in earnest. 1914 brought a large lumber operation and railroad connecting Port Angeles to the more densely populated mainland. Completion of the Hood Canal Bridge in 1961 greatly reduced travel times from Seattle and other population centers to the southeast, bringing a previously unseen level of tourism to the area. Tourism, especially to Olympic National Park, replaced the logging industry and continues to be the main economy to this day.

The Creation of Hot Springs

Local Native American lore tells a story of how Olympic Hot Springs and Sol Duc Hot Springs were formed, and it goes like this: Many years ago there were two mighty dragons. One dragon lived in the Elwha valley while the other lived in the Sol Duc valley. Neither of them knew of the other's existence until one day, while out hunting, they came across each other at the crest of the ridge separating the two valleys. A fierce battle ensued, each dragon blaming the other for invading its territory. The dragons fought a brutal battle, each trying to reclaim their own land. This continued for many years until both dragons acknowledged that they were evenly matched. They turned and flew back down to their respective valleys and crawled into caves. The hot springs we now enjoy are from the tears of these mighty dragons, who still cry from their defeat.

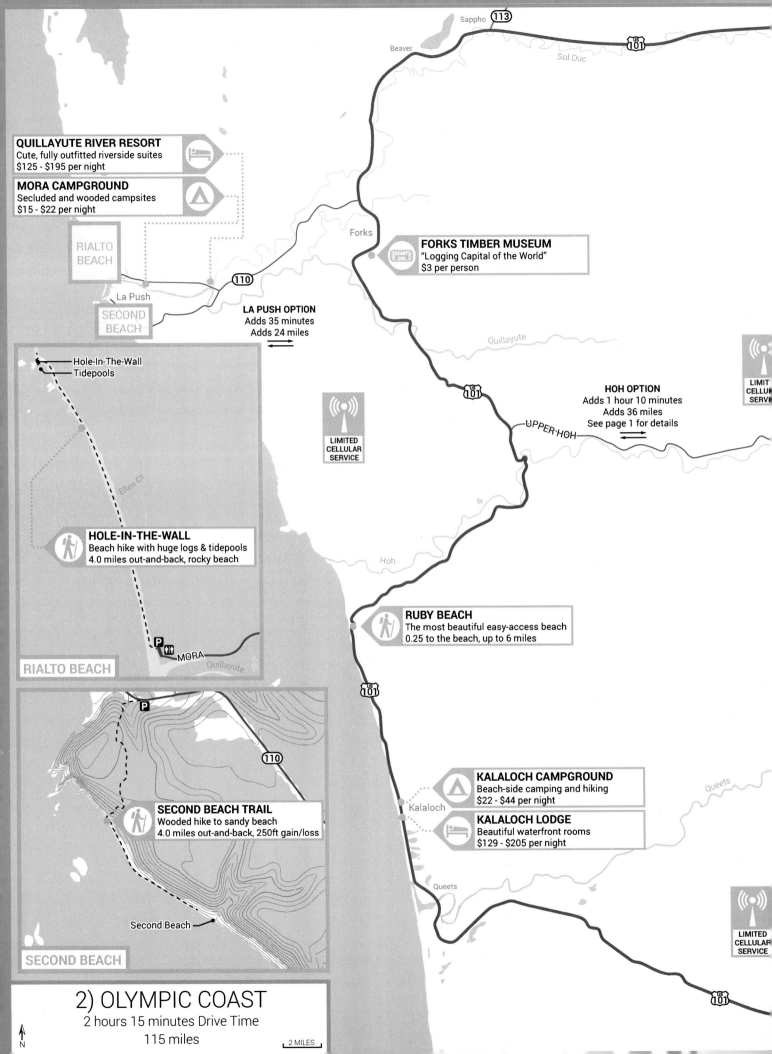

QUILLAYUTE RIVER RESORT
Cute, fully outfitted riverside suites
$125 - $195 per night

MORA CAMPGROUND
Secluded and wooded campsites
$15 - $22 per night

RIALTO
BEACH

La Push

SECOND
BEACH

Sappho

Beaver

Sol Duc

Forks

FORKS TIMBER MUSEUM
"Logging Capital of the World"
$3 per person

LA PUSH OPTION
Adds 35 minutes
Adds 24 miles

Quillayute

Hole-In-The-Wall
Tidepools

Ellen Cr

LIMITED CELLULAR SERVICE

UPPER HOH

HOH OPTION
Adds 1 hour 10 minutes
Adds 36 miles
See page 1 for details

LIMIT
CELLULA
SERVI

HOLE-IN-THE-WALL
Beach hike with huge logs & tidepools
4.0 miles out-and-back, rocky beach

Hoh

MORA

Quillayute

RIALTO BEACH

RUBY BEACH
The most beautiful easy-access beach
0.25 to the beach, up to 6 miles

Queets

SECOND BEACH TRAIL
Wooded hike to sandy beach
4.0 miles out-and-back, 250ft gain/loss

Kalaloch

KALALOCH CAMPGROUND
Beach-side camping and hiking
$22 - $44 per night

KALALOCH LODGE
Beautiful waterfront rooms
$129 - $205 per night

Second Beach

Queets

SECOND BEACH

LIMITED CELLULAR SERVICE

2) OLYMPIC COAST
2 hours 15 minutes Drive Time
115 miles

N

2 MILES

OLYMPIC COAST

Olympic National Park Travel Tips

Olympic National Park is a unique place in many ways. Here you'll find a beautiful trifecta of rugged coast, moss draped rain forest, and glaciated alpine. Unlike most national parks, there are no roads that connect through the park. Instead, the intrepid traveler must circumnavigate and puncture the outskirts where roads are available.

Hurricane Ridge provides roadside access to the high alpine areas and is the most popular place in the park. The road to Hurricane Ridge is open year-round, making it a great snowshoeing destination in the winter. The Hoh rain forest is famous for it huge trees and Tolkien-esque ambiance. The Hoh river trail is the main access route for mountaineers wishing to climb 7,980 foot tall Mount Olympus. The coastline is a mixture of rugged rocky and beautiful sandy beaches. Ruby Beach is the best easy-access beach but some of the true gems, like Shi Shi and Second Beach, require longer hikes.

If you only have a day to visit Olympic National Park, it's best to choose just one region to explore. A full trip around the park required 4 days minimum to see the sights. Of course, the longer you have to spend the better you'll get to know this beautiful place.

Fun Facts about Olympic National Park

1. 95% of the land is designated as Wilderness, one of the highest ratios of any National Park.
2. There are over 3,000 miles of rivers and streams fed by over 60 named glaciers.
3. It's the 4th most-visited park, with almost 4 million annual visitors. Most people come to experience the park's amazing hiking opportunities.
4. There are 3.5x more trail miles than road miles in the park.
5. Mount Olympus, the highest peak on the peninsula, cannot be seen from any metropolitan center including Seattle.
6. The Hoh rain forest receives between 12 to 14 FEET or rain each year! Olympic is home to the only temperate rain forest in the contiguous Unites States.
7. The coastline is 73 miles of beaches, sea stacks, and rocks. One of the best ways to experience the park is by backpacking the entire length.

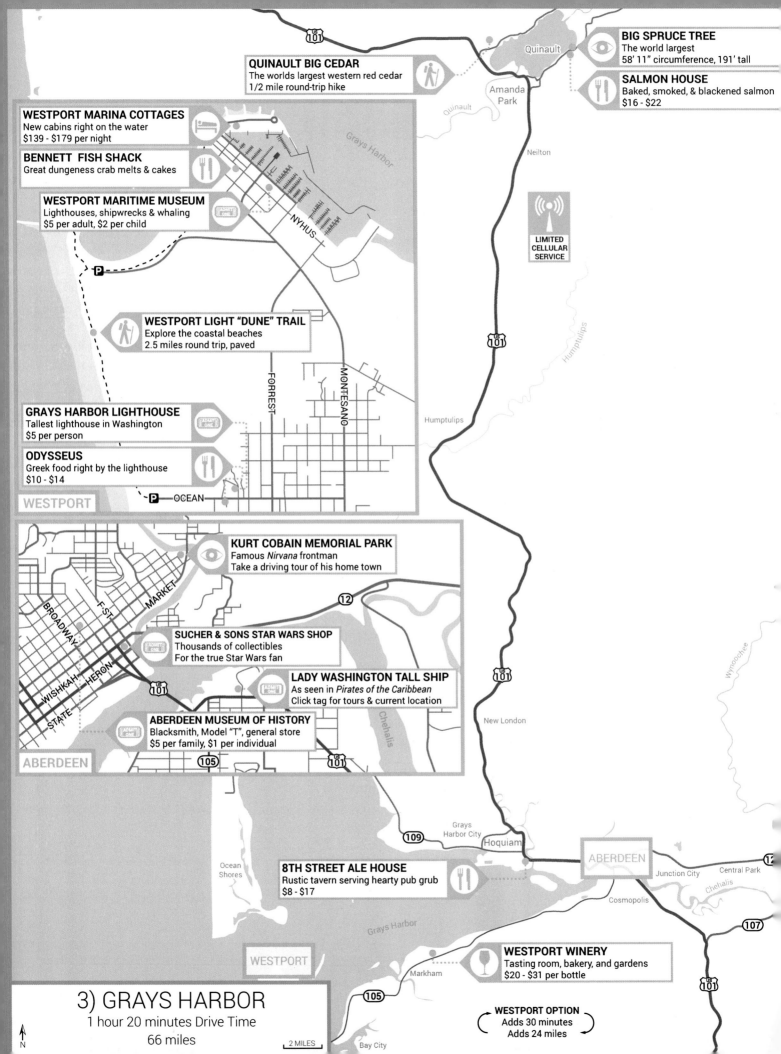

QUINAULT BIG CEDAR
The worlds largest western red cedar
1/2 mile round-trip hike

BIG SPRUCE TREE
The world largest
58' 11" circumference, 191' tall

SALMON HOUSE
Baked, smoked, & blackened salmon
$16 - $22

WESTPORT MARINA COTTAGES
New cabins right on the water
$139 - $179 per night

BENNETT FISH SHACK
Great dungeness crab melts & cakes

WESTPORT MARITIME MUSEUM
Lighthouses, shipwrecks & whaling
$5 per adult, $2 per child

LIMITED CELLULAR SERVICE

WESTPORT LIGHT "DUNE" TRAIL
Explore the coastal beaches
2.5 miles round trip, paved

GRAYS HARBOR LIGHTHOUSE
Tallest lighthouse in Washington
$5 per person

ODYSSEUS
Greek food right by the lighthouse
$10 - $14

WESTPORT

KURT COBAIN MEMORIAL PARK
Famous *Nirvana* frontman
Take a driving tour of his home town

SUCHER & SONS STAR WARS SHOP
Thousands of collectibles
For the true Star Wars fan

LADY WASHINGTON TALL SHIP
As seen in *Pirates of the Caribbean*
Click tag for tours & current location

ABERDEEN MUSEUM OF HISTORY
Blacksmith, Model "T", general store
$5 per family, $1 per individual

ABERDEEN

8TH STREET ALE HOUSE
Rustic tavern serving hearty pub grub
$8 - $17

WESTPORT

WESTPORT WINERY
Tasting room, bakery, and gardens
$20 - $31 per bottle

3) GRAYS HARBOR
1 hour 20 minutes Drive Time
66 miles

2 MILES

WESTPORT OPTION
Adds 30 minutes
Adds 24 miles

GRAYS HARBOR

About Estuaries

Grays Harbor is the third largest ria estuary located along the United States pacific coast (after San Francisco Bay and Willapa Bay). An *estuary* is partly enclosed coastal bay with fresh water flowing into it. This mixture of fresh and salt water creates nutrient rich brackish water, which is why estuaries are one of the most productive natural habitats in the world. A *ria* is a type of coastal inlet formed by a drowned river valley. A treelike outline, caused by smaller valleys stretching outward, is the classic look of a ria. Ria are caused by either global sea levels rising or local land sinking. The final result is a disproportionately large bay for the size of the river.

The Corps of Discovery

On May 14th, 1804, Meriwether Lewis and William Clark began a two and a half year journey from St. Louis to the mouth of the Columbia River. Their task was to chart the land and collect information for future expansion. The Corps of Discovery faced many challenges along their one and a half year trek to the Pacific, but miraculously only lost one man along the way. In mid-November of 1805, the Corps was nearing the mouth of the Columbia. Their hope was to meet up with the last trading ship of the season for valuable supplies and to send their notes back home to President Jefferson. However, on November 10th a fierce storm whipped up, forcing the Corps off the river at a site they named Dismal Nitch. The Corps was trapped here for 6 brutal days, missing their chance to meet up with the trader ship.

Finally, the weather cleared, which allowed the Corps to establish Station Camp and finish their trek to the Pacific. The Corps stayed at Station Camp in order to create an accurate map of the mouth of the Columbia and surrounding region. On November 24th, 1805, cold rains and brutal weather forced the Corps to seek a winter camp with more protection and nearby game than Station Camp could provide. The party crossed the Columbia to the Oregon side and established Fort Clatsop where they spent the winter.

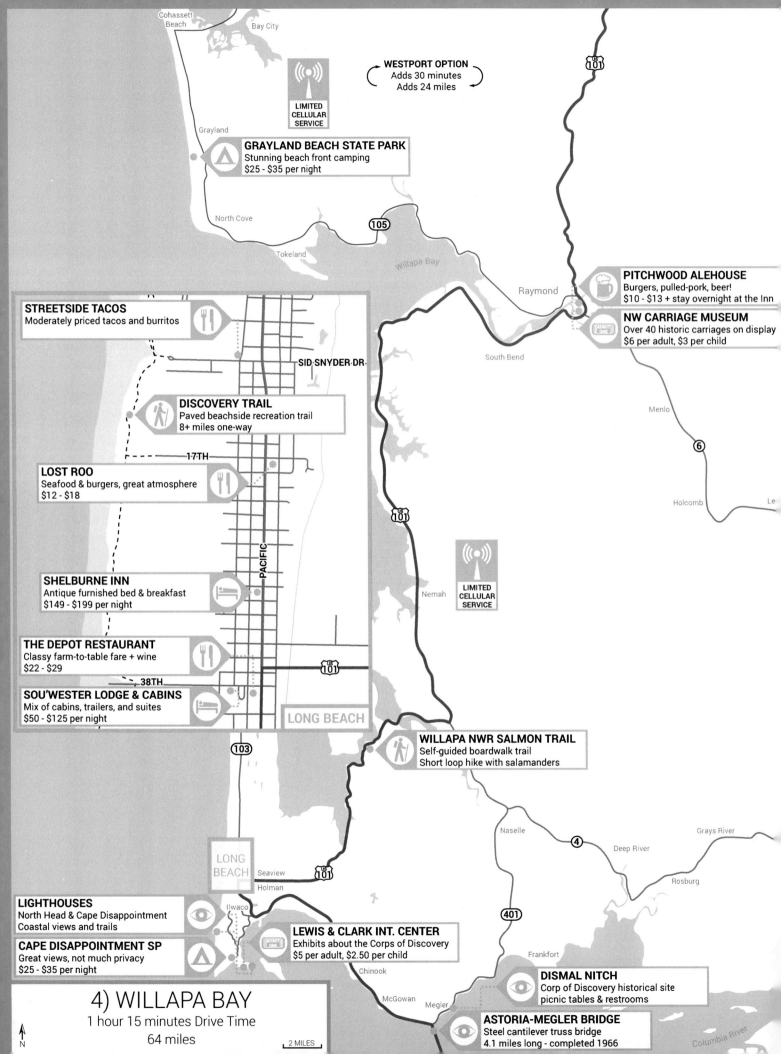

WESTPORT OPTION
Adds 30 minutes
Adds 24 miles

GRAYLAND BEACH STATE PARK
Stunning beach front camping
$25 - $35 per night

LIMITED CELLULAR SERVICE

PITCHWOOD ALEHOUSE
Burgers, pulled-pork, beer!
$10 - $13 + stay overnight at the Inn

NW CARRIAGE MUSEUM
Over 40 historic carriages on display
$6 per adult, $3 per child

STREETSIDE TACOS
Moderately priced tacos and burritos

SID SNYDER DR

DISCOVERY TRAIL
Paved beachside recreation trail
8+ miles one-way

17TH

LOST ROO
Seafood & burgers, great atmosphere
$12 - $18

PACIFIC

LIMITED CELLULAR SERVICE

SHELBURNE INN
Antique furnished bed & breakfast
$149 - $199 per night

THE DEPOT RESTAURANT
Classy farm-to-table fare + wine
$22 - $29

38TH

SOU'WESTER LODGE & CABINS
Mix of cabins, trailers, and suites
$50 - $125 per night

LONG BEACH

WILLAPA NWR SALMON TRAIL
Self-guided boardwalk trail
Short loop hike with salamanders

LONG BEACH
Seaview
Holman

LIGHTHOUSES
North Head & Cape Disappointment
Coastal views and trails

CAPE DISAPPOINTMENT SP
Great views, not much privacy
$25 - $35 per night

Ilwaco

LEWIS & CLARK INT. CENTER
Exhibits about the Corps of Discovery
$5 per adult, $2.50 per child

Frankfort

DISMAL NITCH
Corp of Discovery historical site
picnic tables & restrooms

Chinook

McGowan   Megler

ASTORIA-MEGLER BRIDGE
Steel cantilever truss bridge
4.1 miles long - completed 1966

4) WILLAPA BAY
1 hour 15 minutes Drive Time
64 miles

2 MILES

N

Columbia River

WILLAPA BAY

Long Beach: Local Advice from Carol Zahorsky

This 28-mile finger of sand has long been a vacation destination for Portland families and Seattleites. Long Beach is known for a concentration of outstanding restaurants which draw inspiration and ingredients from...

- Willapa Bay - oysters & butter clams
- Columbia River - dungeness crab
- Pacific Ocean - salmon, tuna, & halibut
- Willapa Hills & Fields - chanterelle, matsutake, porcini
- and Bogs - cranberries

Miles and miles of wide, sandy public beach, an ocean-front paved interpretive trail, a boardwalk, lighthouses, parks, museums, and charming communities make it Washington's most prized beach destination.

NOT TO BE MISSED
- The 120-year old Shelburne Inn, Restaurant, and Pub
- The Chef's Table at The Depot Restaurant
- The view & music at Pickled Fish
- The restored vintage trailers at The Sou'wester
- 42nd Street Cafe

Carol Zahorsky has been sharing her favorite experiences on the Long Beach Peninsula and elsewhere in Washington with visitors and guests for 20 years. With a love of words, spacious outdoors, deftly prepared fresh food and world travel, she works as a communications professional in the Seattle/Portland region.

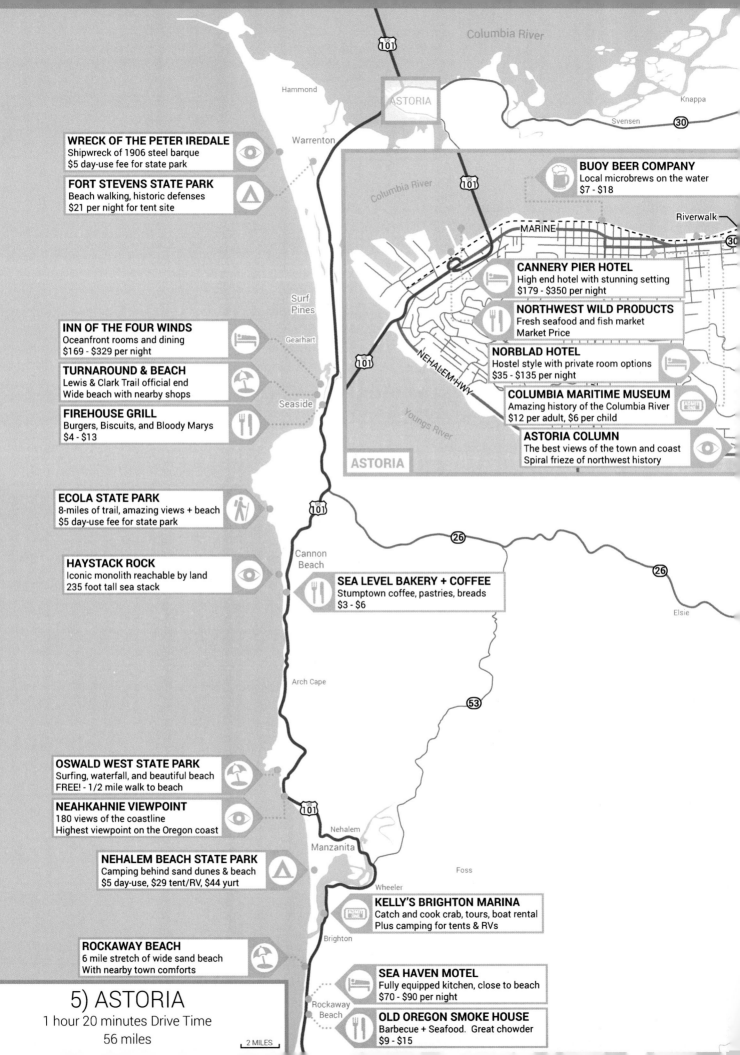

WRECK OF THE PETER IREDALE
Shipwreck of 1906 steel barque
$5 day-use fee for state park

FORT STEVENS STATE PARK
Beach walking, historic defenses
$21 per night for tent site

BUOY BEER COMPANY
Local microbrews on the water
$7 - $18

CANNERY PIER HOTEL
High end hotel with stunning setting
$179 - $350 per night

NORTHWEST WILD PRODUCTS
Fresh seafood and fish market
Market Price

INN OF THE FOUR WINDS
Oceanfront rooms and dining
$169 - $329 per night

NORBLAD HOTEL
Hostel style with private room options
$35 - $135 per night

TURNAROUND & BEACH
Lewis & Clark Trail official end
Wide beach with nearby shops

COLUMBIA MARITIME MUSEUM
Amazing history of the Columbia River
$12 per adult, $6 per child

FIREHOUSE GRILL
Burgers, Biscuits, and Bloody Marys
$4 - $13

ASTORIA COLUMN
The best views of the town and coast
Spiral frieze of northwest history

ASTORIA

ECOLA STATE PARK
8-miles of trail, amazing views + beach
$5 day-use fee for state park

HAYSTACK ROCK
Iconic monolith reachable by land
235 foot tall sea stack

SEA LEVEL BAKERY + COFFEE
Stumptown coffee, pastries, breads
$3 - $6

OSWALD WEST STATE PARK
Surfing, waterfall, and beautiful beach
FREE! - 1/2 mile walk to beach

NEAHKAHNIE VIEWPOINT
180 views of the coastline
Highest viewpoint on the Oregon coast

NEHALEM BEACH STATE PARK
Camping behind sand dunes & beach
$5 day-use, $29 tent/RV, $44 yurt

KELLY'S BRIGHTON MARINA
Catch and cook crab, tours, boat rental
Plus camping for tents & RVs

ROCKAWAY BEACH
6 mile stretch of wide sand beach
With nearby town comforts

SEA HAVEN MOTEL
Fully equipped kitchen, close to beach
$70 - $90 per night

5) ASTORIA
1 hour 20 minutes Drive Time
56 miles

2 MILES

OLD OREGON SMOKE HOUSE
Barbecue + Seafood. Great chowder
$9 - $15

N

OREGON

The Oregon coastline is arguably the best stretch of road along the Pacific Coast - there is no other section of Highway 101 or 1 that stays so consistently close to the ocean. Rugged headlands, large rivers, and quiet beach towns are found throughout the entire coast. There is so much to explore with very few population centers close by, which means everything feels relaxed and local.

Along this stretch of Highway 101 you can expect to find delicious cheese factories, amazing micro-breweries, scrumptious seafood, and plenty of charmingly quirky motels and bed & breakfasts.

ASTORIA

The Mighty Columbia River

The Columbia is the fourth largest river by volume in North America, and the largest by volume to enter the Pacific. Over the course of 1243 miles this river drops 2690 feet from Columbia Lake, British Columbia to Astoria, Oregon. For over 15,000 years native tribes fished, traveled, and traded along the Columbia River. Salmon served as both a major source of food and also as a focal point of their religious beliefs. Many historic fishing sites, such as Celilo Falls, were submerged when hydroelectric dams were built.

In the area known as Columbia Bar, where the river meets the ocean, conditions change from calm to life-threatening in a matter of minutes. Over 2000 ships and 700 live have been lost in this one area alone, giving it the nickname Graveyard of the Pacific.

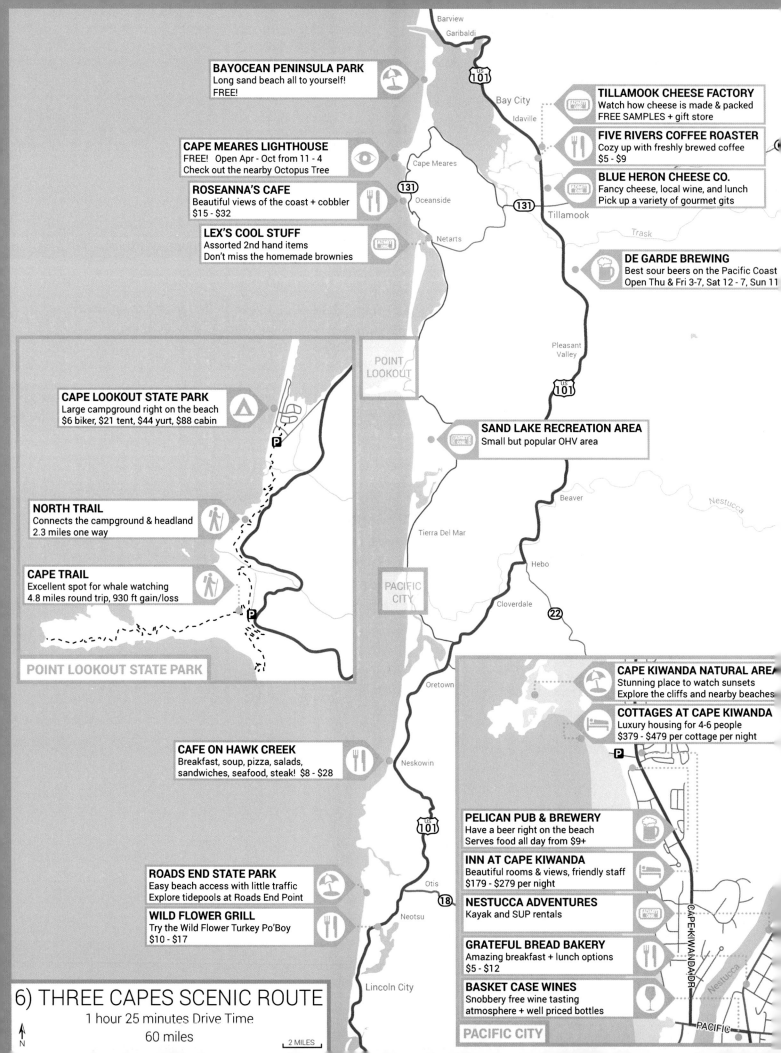

BAYOCEAN PENINSULA PARK
Long sand beach all to yourself!
FREE!

TILLAMOOK CHEESE FACTORY
Watch how cheese is made & packed
FREE SAMPLES + gift store

FIVE RIVERS COFFEE ROASTER
Cozy up with freshly brewed coffee
$5 - $9

BLUE HERON CHEESE CO.
Fancy cheese, local wine, and lunch
Pick up a variety of gourmet gifts

CAPE MEARES LIGHTHOUSE
FREE! Open Apr - Oct from 11 - 4
Check out the nearby Octopus Tree

ROSEANNA'S CAFE
Beautiful views of the coast + cobbler
$15 - $32

LEX'S COOL STUFF
Assorted 2nd hand items
Don't miss the homemade brownies

DE GARDE BREWING
Best sour beers on the Pacific Coast
Open Thu & Fri 3-7, Sat 12 - 7, Sun 11

CAPE LOOKOUT STATE PARK
Large campground right on the beach
$6 biker, $21 tent, $44 yurt, $88 cabin

SAND LAKE RECREATION AREA
Small but popular OHV area

NORTH TRAIL
Connects the campground & headland
2.3 miles one way

CAPE TRAIL
Excellent spot for whale watching
4.8 miles round trip, 930 ft gain/loss

POINT LOOKOUT STATE PARK

CAPE KIWANDA NATURAL AREA
Stunning place to watch sunsets
Explore the cliffs and nearby beaches

COTTAGES AT CAPE KIWANDA
Luxury housing for 4-6 people
$379 - $479 per cottage per night

CAFE ON HAWK CREEK
Breakfast, soup, pizza, salads,
sandwiches, seafood, steak! $8 - $28

PELICAN PUB & BREWERY
Have a beer right on the beach
Serves food all day from $9+

INN AT CAPE KIWANDA
Beautiful rooms & views, friendly staff
$179 - $279 per night

ROADS END STATE PARK
Easy beach access with little traffic
Explore tidepools at Roads End Point

WILD FLOWER GRILL
Try the Wild Flower Turkey Po'Boy
$10 - $17

NESTUCCA ADVENTURES
Kayak and SUP rentals

GRATEFUL BREAD BAKERY
Amazing breakfast + lunch options
$5 - $12

BASKET CASE WINES
Snobbery free wine tasting
atmosphere + well priced bottles

6) THREE CAPES SCENIC ROUTE
1 hour 25 minutes Drive Time
60 miles

2 MILES

PACIFIC CITY

THREE CAPES SCENIC ROUTE

5 Absolutely Cannot Pass-Up Destinations: Local Advice from Skyler Lanning

1) Ecola State Park is a great hiking destination, with old growth rain forest and fantastic trails hugging the cape. The trails also offer great views of the crashing surf below, with numerous vantage points looking directly onto the famous Haystack Rock.

2) Neahkahnie Overlook is the highest viewpoint along the Oregon Coast and uses this to full effect - it offers visitors enormous 180 degree views of the coastline. On a clear day, common sights are the town of Manzanita, Nehalem Bay, Tillamook Bay and the Three Arch Rocks.

3) Manzanita which mean "Little Apple," is a very cute and quaint coastal town that makes for a great stop. They have a cool coffee shop, aptly named Manzanita Coffee Shop, a number of confectionary shops, and a very stroll-able main street.

4) The Tillamook Cheese Factory is a great stop for locals and tourists alike. It is a cooperative-owned cheese maker that produces 40 million pounds of cheese annually. They offer self-guided tours of their production lines, complimentary cheese tastings, and amazing ice cream for purchase.

5) Whale watching is always in season along the Oregon Coast, due to a permanent whale population numbering around 40. Peak viewing is usually in June and December, with whale watchers trying to catch glimpses of the thousands of whales on their annual migration. Regardless of the time of year, Depot Bay and their whale-watching center is a fantastic stop to catch sightings. Interesting side note - the city also has the world's smallest harbor.

Skyler Lanning and his wife Maria operate Wildwood Adventures, a day tour company out of Portland, OR. They offer public and customized tours to some of Oregon's greatest natural treasures. For more information visit www.WildwoodTours.com

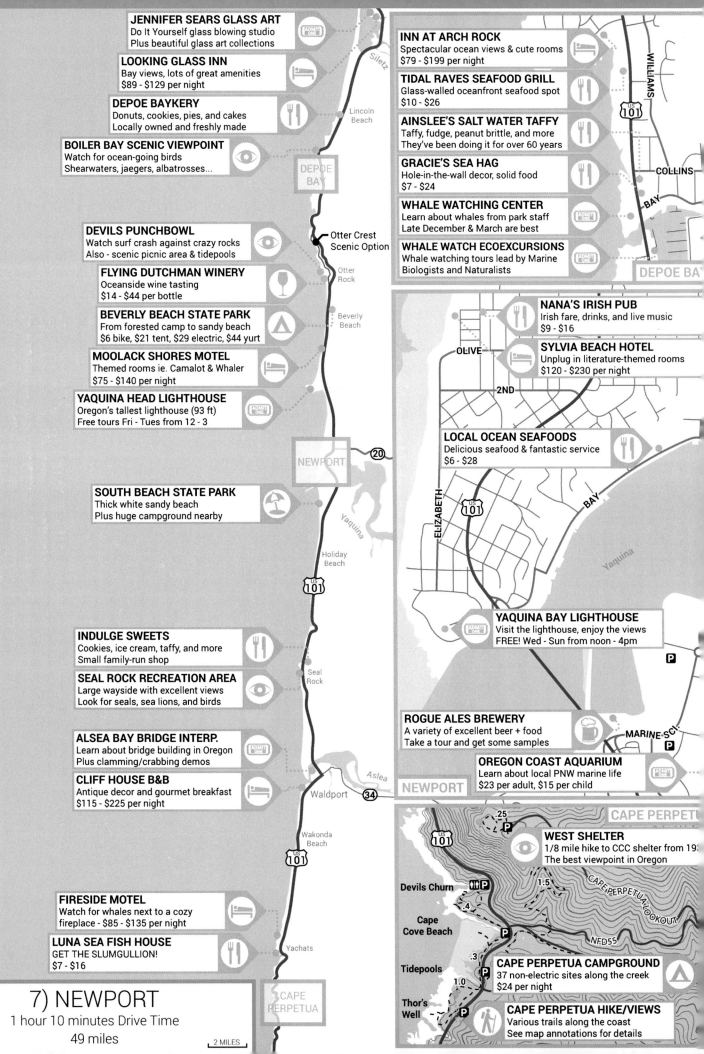

JENNIFER SEARS GLASS ART
Do It Yourself glass blowing studio
Plus beautiful glass art collections

LOOKING GLASS INN
Bay views, lots of great amenities
$89 - $129 per night

DEPOE BAYKERY
Donuts, cookies, pies, and cakes
Locally owned and freshly made

BOILER BAY SCENIC VIEWPOINT
Watch for ocean-going birds
Shearwaters, jaegers, albatrosses...

DEVILS PUNCHBOWL
Watch surf crash against crazy rocks
Also - scenic picnic area & tidepools

FLYING DUTCHMAN WINERY
Oceanside wine tasting
$14 - $44 per bottle

BEVERLY BEACH STATE PARK
From forested camp to sandy beach
$6 bike, $21 tent, $29 electric, $44 yurt

MOOLACK SHORES MOTEL
Themed rooms ie. Camalot & Whaler
$75 - $140 per night

YAQUINA HEAD LIGHTHOUSE
Oregon's tallest lighthouse (93 ft)
Free tours Fri - Tues from 12 - 3

SOUTH BEACH STATE PARK
Thick white sandy beach
Plus huge campground nearby

INDULGE SWEETS
Cookies, ice cream, taffy, and more
Small family-run shop

SEAL ROCK RECREATION AREA
Large wayside with excellent views
Look for seals, sea lions, and birds

ALSEA BAY BRIDGE INTERP.
Learn about bridge building in Oregon
Plus clamming/crabbing demos

CLIFF HOUSE B&B
Antique decor and gourmet breakfast
$115 - $225 per night

FIRESIDE MOTEL
Watch for whales next to a cozy
fireplace - $85 - $135 per night

LUNA SEA FISH HOUSE
GET THE SLUMGULLION!
$7 - $16

7) NEWPORT
1 hour 10 minutes Drive Time
49 miles

2 MILES

INN AT ARCH ROCK
Spectacular ocean views & cute rooms
$79 - $199 per night

TIDAL RAVES SEAFOOD GRILL
Glass-walled oceanfront seafood spot
$10 - $26

AINSLEE'S SALT WATER TAFFY
Taffy, fudge, peanut brittle, and more
They've been doing it for over 60 years

GRACIE'S SEA HAG
Hole-in-the-wall decor, solid food
$7 - $24

WHALE WATCHING CENTER
Learn about whales from park staff
Late December & March are best

WHALE WATCH ECOEXCURSIONS
Whale watching tours lead by Marine
Biologists and Naturalists

NANA'S IRISH PUB
Irish fare, drinks, and live music
$9 - $16

SYLVIA BEACH HOTEL
Unplug in literature-themed rooms
$120 - $230 per night

LOCAL OCEAN SEAFOODS
Delicious seafood & fantastic service
$6 - $28

YAQUINA BAY LIGHTHOUSE
Visit the lighthouse, enjoy the views
FREE! Wed - Sun from noon - 4pm

ROGUE ALES BREWERY
A variety of excellent beer + food
Take a tour and get some samples

OREGON COAST AQUARIUM
Learn about local PNW marine life
$23 per adult, $15 per child

WEST SHELTER
1/8 mile hike to CCC shelter from 19?
The best viewpoint in Oregon

CAPE PERPETUA CAMPGROUND
37 non-electric sites along the creek
$24 per night

CAPE PERPETUA HIKE/VIEWS
Various trails along the coast
See map annotations for details

The Three Capes: Local Advice from Jeremy Strober

The best stop along Highway 101 in Oregon requires that you veer off of Highway 101 by just 3 miles. The Three Capes Scenic Route begins just south of Cloverdale and takes you to Pacific City where you'll find Cape Kiwanda, the southernmost Cape along the Three Capes Route.

In Pacific City, you will find the lesser-known Haystack Rock, towering 357 feet above the water. Adjacent to the Cape, it makes for beautiful eye-candy as you stare west.

Sitting right on the beach at Cape Kiwanda is the Pelican Pub & Brewery, one of the state's award-winning breweries. The Pelican offers breakfast, lunch, and dinner on an outdoor patio so you can enjoy the beach al fresco.

The Cape provides for some of the most diverse activities along the coast. It is the Home of the Dory Fleet, a flat-bottom fishing boat that launches off the sand into the surf and has done so from this spot for over 100 years. It is one of the best surfing spots along the coast, providing perfect breakers courtesy of the sandbar that stretches from the Rock to the Cape. Kayakers launch here to fish or ride the waves. The marine garden provides tidepooling galore. And the 18 story sand dune creates a mecca for climbing, running, jumping, and sand boarding.

You can reconnect to Highway 101 as you travel north, after visiting Cape Lookout and Cape Meares.

As the operator of three local lodging establishments, Jeremy Stober often gets asked about the unique places to eat, drink, and visit. Being able to recommend the perfect match to a guest's desire is his favorite part of the hospitality business! Find out more at www.yourlittlebeachtown.com

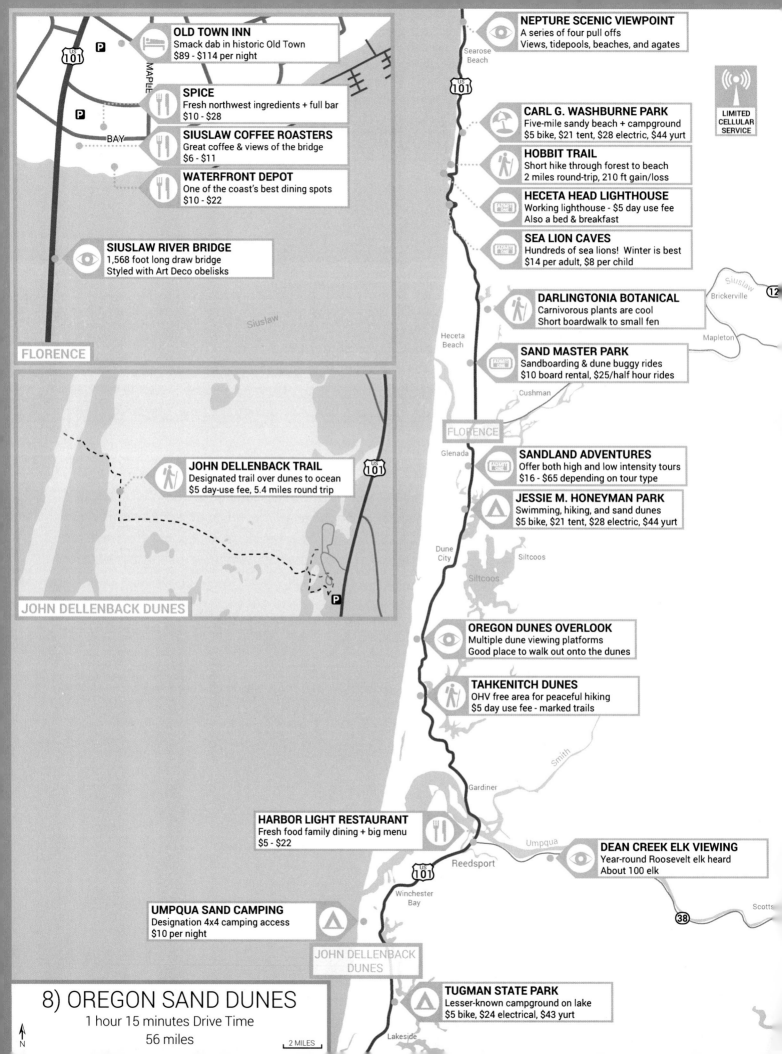

OLD TOWN INN
Smack dab in historic Old Town
$89 - $114 per night

SPICE
Fresh northwest ingredients + full bar
$10 - $28

SIUSLAW COFFEE ROASTERS
Great coffee & views of the bridge
$6 - $11

WATERFRONT DEPOT
One of the coast's best dining spots
$10 - $22

SIUSLAW RIVER BRIDGE
1,568 foot long draw bridge
Styled with Art Deco obelisks

FLORENCE

JOHN DELLENBACK TRAIL
Designated trail over dunes to ocean
$5 day-use fee, 5.4 miles round trip

JOHN DELLENBACK DUNES

NEPTURE SCENIC VIEWPOINT
A series of four pull offs
Views, tidepools, beaches, and agates

Searose Beach

LIMITED CELLULAR SERVICE

CARL G. WASHBURNE PARK
Five-mile sandy beach + campground
$5 bike, $21 tent, $28 electric, $44 yurt

HOBBIT TRAIL
Short hike through forest to beach
2 miles round-trip, 210 ft gain/loss

HECETA HEAD LIGHTHOUSE
Working lighthouse - $5 day use fee
Also a bed & breakfast

SEA LION CAVES
Hundreds of sea lions! Winter is best
$14 per adult, $8 per child

Siuslaw

Brickerville

Mapleton

DARLINGTONIA BOTANICAL
Carnivorous plants are cool
Short boardwalk to small fen

Heceta Beach

SAND MASTER PARK
Sandboarding & dune buggy rides
$10 board rental, $25/half hour rides

Cushman

FLORENCE

Glenada

SANDLAND ADVENTURES
Offer both high and low intensity tours
$16 - $65 depending on tour type

JESSIE M. HONEYMAN PARK
Swimming, hiking, and sand dunes
$5 bike, $21 tent, $28 electric, $44 yurt

Dune City

Siltcoos

Siltcoos

OREGON DUNES OVERLOOK
Multiple dune viewing platforms
Good place to walk out onto the dunes

TAHKENITCH DUNES
OHV free area for peaceful hiking
$5 day use fee - marked trails

Smith

Gardiner

HARBOR LIGHT RESTAURANT
Fresh food family dining + big menu
$5 - $22

Umpqua

DEAN CREEK ELK VIEWING
Year-round Roosevelt elk heard
About 100 elk

Reedsport

Winchester Bay

Scotts

UMPQUA SAND CAMPING
Designation 4x4 camping access
$10 per night

JOHN DELLENBACK DUNES

8) OREGON SAND DUNES
1 hour 15 minutes Drive Time
56 miles

N

2 MILES

TUGMAN STATE PARK
Lesser-known campground on lake
$5 bike, $24 electrical, $43 yurt

Lakeside

OREGON SAND DUNES

Florence: Local Advice from Stephen Hoshaw

Nestled along Highway 101, Florence is well suited for all types of adventure. With long sandy beaches and dunes, scenic viewpoints, and rocky coastal panoramas, this might be one of the best places to experience the Oregon Coast.

Search for coastal wildlife while whale watching from Heceta Head Lighthouse scenic viewpoint. Or venture underground at the Sea Lion Caves to hear the echo of barking sea lions.

At the Oregon Dunes National Recreation Area and Sand Master Park thrill-seeking adventurers can choose between sandboarding or riding in dune buggies between the massive hills of sand.

Florence's Old Town district offers boutique shopping experiences and cozy coastal meals at local hotspots like Bridgewater Ocean Fresh Fish House and Waterfront Depot.

Stephen grew up in the Northwest and has fond memories of both week-long family reunions at the Coast, and quick day trips from Eugene with friends. Learn more at www.eugenecascadescoast.org

Formation of Sand Dunes

The combination of desert sands, old growth forests, lakes, and ocean found at Oregon Sand Dunes is unique to the southern Oregon coast. By why is it here?

12 million years ago, uplifting layers of sedimentary rock formed what is now the Oregon Coastal Range mountains. As these mountains eroded, the soft rocks traveled downstream and were broken into small granular pieces. These sediments were then deposited at the mouth of the rivers along a gently sloping marine layer called the Coos Bay Dune Sheet. Unlike the headlands found to the north and south, this flat sandstone bottom allows for sands to be picked up and deposited by waves along the shorelines. Finally, these sands were picked up by the wind and dropped over 2.5 miles inland to form the dunes.

Over thousands of year, the dunes have been shaped by wind and water into a vast array of shapes and sizes.

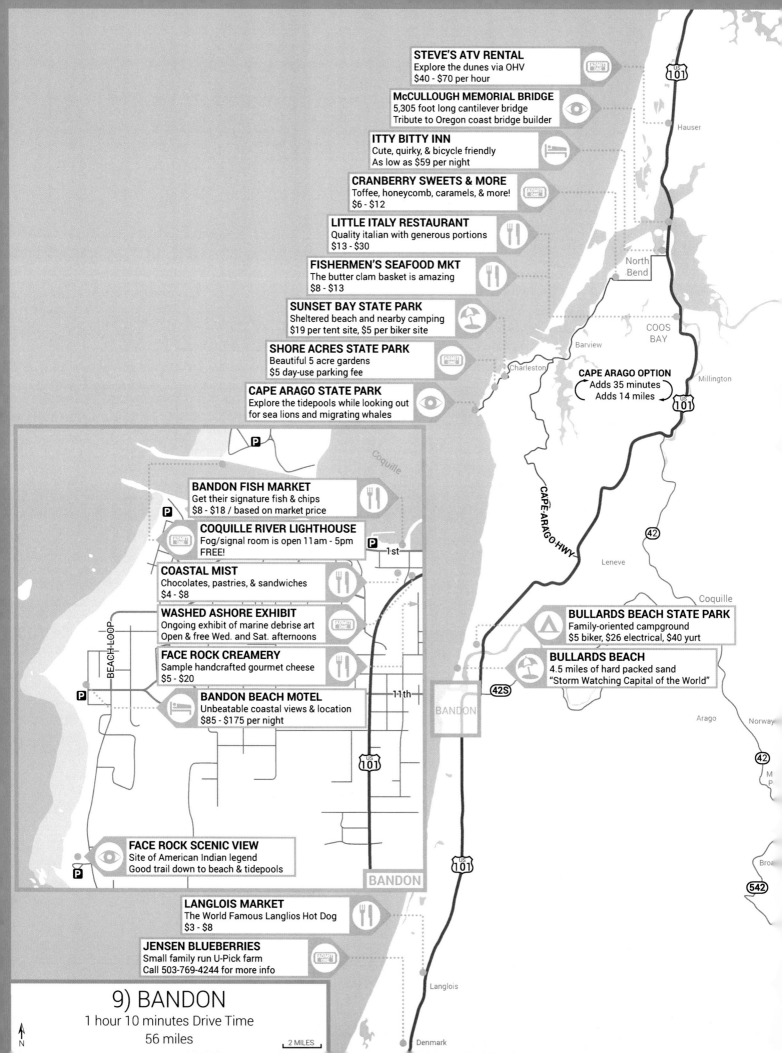

STEVE'S ATV RENTAL
Explore the dunes via OHV
$40 - $70 per hour

McCULLOUGH MEMORIAL BRIDGE
5,305 foot long cantilever bridge
Tribute to Oregon coast bridge builder

ITTY BITTY INN
Cute, quirky, & bicycle friendly
As low as $59 per night

CRANBERRY SWEETS & MORE
Toffee, honeycomb, caramels, & more!
$6 - $12

LITTLE ITALY RESTAURANT
Quality italian with generous portions
$13 - $30

FISHERMEN'S SEAFOOD MKT
The butter clam basket is amazing
$8 - $13

SUNSET BAY STATE PARK
Sheltered beach and nearby camping
$19 per tent site, $5 per biker site

SHORE ACRES STATE PARK
Beautiful 5 acre gardens
$5 day-use parking fee

CAPE ARAGO STATE PARK
Explore the tidepools while looking out
for sea lions and migrating whales

CAPE ARAGO OPTION
Adds 35 minutes
Adds 14 miles

BANDON FISH MARKET
Get their signature fish & chips
$8 - $18 / based on market price

COQUILLE RIVER LIGHTHOUSE
Fog/signal room is open 11am - 5pm
FREE!

COASTAL MIST
Chocolates, pastries, & sandwiches
$4 - $8

WASHED ASHORE EXHIBIT
Ongoing exhibit of marine debrise art
Open & free Wed. and Sat. afternoons

FACE ROCK CREAMERY
Sample handcrafted gourmet cheese
$5 - $20

BANDON BEACH MOTEL
Unbeatable coastal views & location
$85 - $175 per night

BULLARDS BEACH STATE PARK
Family-oriented campground
$5 biker, $26 electrical, $40 yurt

BULLARDS BEACH
4.5 miles of hard packed sand
"Storm Watching Capital of the World"

FACE ROCK SCENIC VIEW
Site of American Indian legend
Good trail down to beach & tidepools

LANGLOIS MARKET
The World Famous Langlios Hot Dog
$3 - $8

JENSEN BLUEBERRIES
Small family run U-Pick farm
Call 503-769-4244 for more info

9) BANDON
1 hour 10 minutes Drive Time
56 miles

2 MILES

N

BANDON

The Legend of Face Rock

Many years ago, the great chief Siskiyou of the mountain tribes planned a visit to four coastal tribes. His daughter Ewauna was to accompany him, which was a great honor. Chief Necomah, being the strongest of the four coastal Chiefs, decided that as a group they would host the greatest potlatch as a show of respect and of their own prosperity.

The days leading up to the potlatch were full of preparation. Necomah ordered massive amounts of clams and mussels to be harvested and stored for the meal. The Elks tribe brought a hundred salmon, cleaned and ready to be roasted. The Sixes brought meat from a dozen elks. The Rogues carried in twenty horses loaded with deer meat. Armed warriors stood guard on the bluff watching for Seatka, the evil spirit of the sea.

Chief Siskiyou arrived with his daughter, who had never before seen the sea. She was enthralled by its beauty despite being warned not to wander near it for fear Seatka would snatch her. With her was her loyal dog Komax and her cat with kittens.

On the morning of the second day, everyone convened in beautiful regalia and commenced the feast. They celebrated this unique visit while eating until they were too tired, at which point they proceeded to sleep in place. Ewauna, wishing to see more of the sea, slipped away from the sleeping camp. A full moon shown down on her as she played at the edge of the ocean.

Finally, she set her basket of kittens down and told Komax to keep watch. Ewauna ran out into the ocean and dove in the crashing surf. She swam for a long time and was slowly pulled away from shore. She was so enraptured that she was unable to hear Komax barking a warning.

Suddenly, the moon became blocked by a dark hand as the fearsome creature Seatka emerged from the water. Komax grabbed the basket of kittens and swam out to help Ewauna. He sunk his sharp teeth into Seatka but was swatted away, along with the basket. Seatka tried to make Ewauna look at him, for his power lived in his gaze, but she stubbornly look straight up at the moon.

Chief Siskiyou rose at sunrise, alarmed to find his daughter missing. Everyone rushed to the sea, only to find Ewauna stubbornly staring up towards the moon with Seatka still trying to meet her gaze. Eventually she turned into stone and you can still see her face gazing up toward the moon to this day.

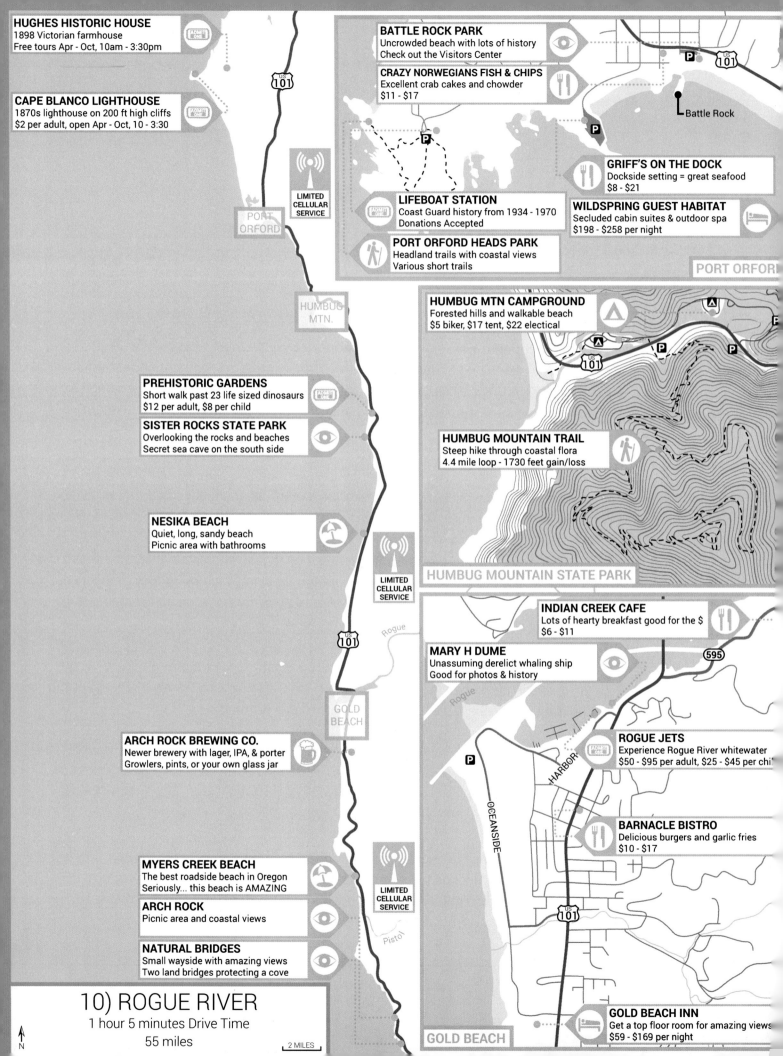

HUGHES HISTORIC HOUSE
1898 Victorian farmhouse
Free tours Apr - Oct, 10am - 3:30pm

CAPE BLANCO LIGHTHOUSE
1870s lighthouse on 200 ft high cliffs
$2 per adult, open Apr - Oct, 10 - 3:30

LIMITED CELLULAR SERVICE

PORT ORFORD

BATTLE ROCK PARK
Uncrowded beach with lots of history
Check out the Visitors Center

CRAZY NORWEGIANS FISH & CHIPS
Excellent crab cakes and chowder
$11 - $17

Battle Rock

GRIFF'S ON THE DOCK
Dockside setting = great seafood
$8 - $21

WILDSPRING GUEST HABITAT
Secluded cabin suites & outdoor spa
$198 - $258 per night

LIFEBOAT STATION
Coast Guard history from 1934 - 1970
Donations Accepted

PORT ORFORD HEADS PARK
Headland trails with coastal views
Various short trails

PORT ORFORD

HUMBUG MTN.

HUMBUG MTN CAMPGROUND
Forested hills and walkable beach
$5 biker, $17 tent, $22 electical

PREHISTORIC GARDENS
Short walk past 23 life sized dinosaurs
$12 per adult, $8 per child

SISTER ROCKS STATE PARK
Overlooking the rocks and beaches
Secret sea cave on the south side

HUMBUG MOUNTAIN TRAIL
Steep hike through coastal flora
4.4 mile loop - 1730 feet gain/loss

NESIKA BEACH
Quiet, long, sandy beach
Picnic area with bathrooms

LIMITED CELLULAR SERVICE

HUMBUG MOUNTAIN STATE PARK

Rogue

INDIAN CREEK CAFE
Lots of hearty breakfast good for the $
$6 - $11

MARY H DUME
Unassuming derelict whaling ship
Good for photos & history

595

Rogue

GOLD BEACH

ARCH ROCK BREWING CO.
Newer brewery with lager, IPA, & porter
Growlers, pints, or your own glass jar

ROGUE JETS
Experience Rogue River whitewater
$50 - $95 per adult, $25 - $45 per chi

HARBOR

BARNACLE BISTRO
Delicious burgers and garlic fries
$10 - $17

OCEANSIDE

MYERS CREEK BEACH
The best roadside beach in Oregon
Seriously... this beach is AMAZING

ARCH ROCK
Picnic area and coastal views

NATURAL BRIDGES
Small wayside with amazing views
Two land bridges protecting a cove

LIMITED CELLULAR SERVICE

Pistol

10) ROGUE RIVER
1 hour 5 minutes Drive Time
55 miles

2 MILES

N

GOLD BEACH

GOLD BEACH INN
Get a top floor room for amazing views
$59 - $169 per night

ROGUE RIVER

Conde McCullough - Bridge Builder

In the early 20th century, towns along the rugged Oregon coast were practically unreachable. By the 1920s, rapidly growing interest in coastal tourism prompted the funding of a highway that would span the entire length. Over the course of five years, from 1921 to 1926, section by section of Highway 101 was completed. Among the many challenges the engineers faced were the many rivers that ran from the Coastal Range Mountains to the ocean. Ferries were commonly used to transport cars and good across the rivers, but they couldn't keep up with the increasing demands the highway brought. Instead, it was decided that bridges must connect each section of road.

Conde McCullough, the Oregon state bridge engineer at the time, was presented with the opportunity to design and build the infrastructure for these key links to the highway. McCullough wasn't just interested in making the bridges structurally sound, but also architecturally beautiful. Over the course of fifteen years, McCullough designed a total of fourteen bridges along Highway 101. These bridges are constructed in a variety of styles and materials. You will find them adorned with Gothic spires, art deco obelisks, and Romanesque arches.

Some notable bridges include the Yaquina Bay Bridge (Newport), the Siuslaw River Bridge (Florence), and the Old Youngs Bay Bridge (Astoria).

McCullough went on to help design over 600 bridges in his lifetime.

Wild and Scenic Rivers

The Rogue River travels 215 miles and over 1 mile in elevation from its source in Crater Lake National Park to the Pacific Ocean at Gold Beach. This river is famous for its stellar whitewater rafting, salmon runs, and outdoor recreation opportunities. The Rogue was one of the original eight river listed under the 1968 National Wild and Scenic Rivers Act. This act focuses on the need to protect our rivers as pristine and scenic areas. Since the inception of the act, over 203 rivers have been granted this status.

Dams have been a controversial topic along the Rogue for over a hundred years. Many dams were originally built to provide hydroelectric power and prevent flooding. However, even with fish ladders designed into the dams, salmon populations dropped dramatically. Numerous dams have been constructed and then demolished -- one was even dynamited by a group of angry commercial fishermen! Now only the William L. Jess Dam remains, which is located 157 miles from the mouth of the river.

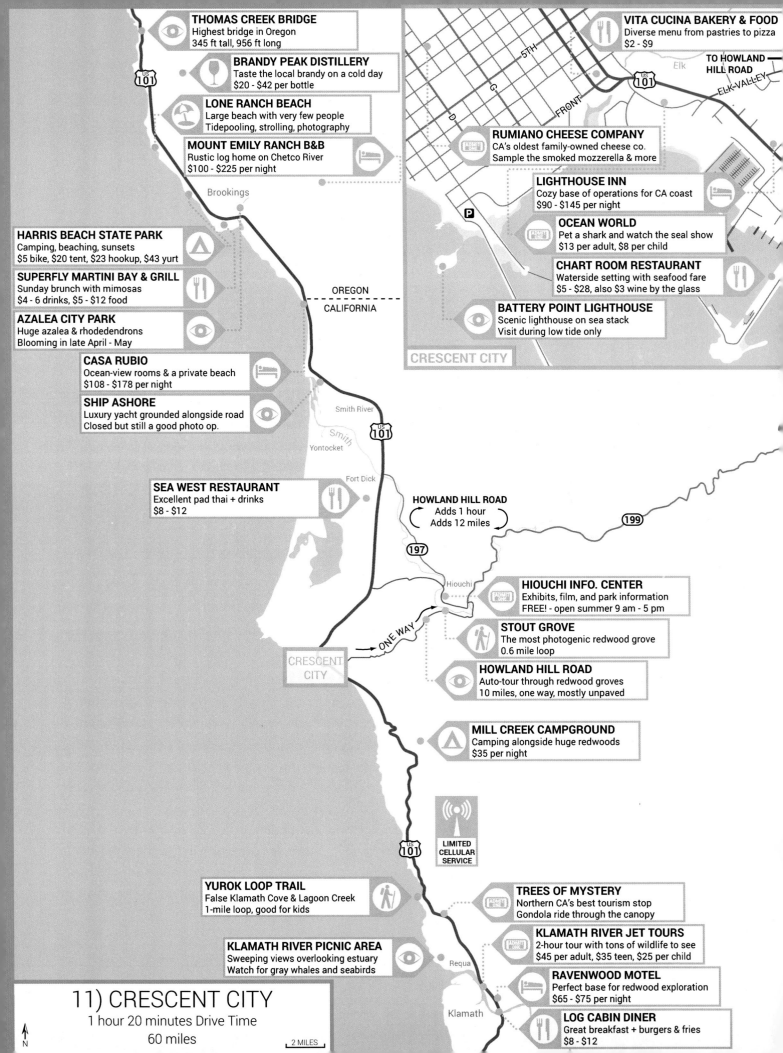

THOMAS CREEK BRIDGE
Highest bridge in Oregon
345 ft tall, 956 ft long

BRANDY PEAK DISTILLERY
Taste the local brandy on a cold day
$20 - $42 per bottle

LONE RANCH BEACH
Large beach with very few people
Tidepooling, strolling, photography

MOUNT EMILY RANCH B&B
Rustic log home on Chetco River
$100 - $225 per night

Brookings

HARRIS BEACH STATE PARK
Camping, beaching, sunsets
$5 bike, $20 tent, $23 hookup, $43 yurt

SUPERFLY MARTINI BAY & GRILL
Sunday brunch with mimosas
$4 - 6 drinks, $5 - $12 food

AZALEA CITY PARK
Huge azalea & rhodedendrons
Blooming in late April - May

OREGON
CALIFORNIA

CASA RUBIO
Ocean-view rooms & a private beach
$108 - $178 per night

SHIP ASHORE
Luxury yacht grounded alongside road
Closed but still a good photo op.

Smith River

Smith

Yontocket

Fort Dick

SEA WEST RESTAURANT
Excellent pad thai + drinks
$8 - $12

HOWLAND HILL ROAD
Adds 1 hour
Adds 12 miles

199

197

Hiouchi

HIOUCHI INFO. CENTER
Exhibits, film, and park information
FREE! - open summer 9 am - 5 pm

ONE WAY

CRESCENT
CITY

STOUT GROVE
The most photogenic redwood grove
0.6 mile loop

HOWLAND HILL ROAD
Auto-tour through redwood groves
10 miles, one way, mostly unpaved

MILL CREEK CAMPGROUND
Camping alongside huge redwoods
$35 per night

**LIMITED
CELLULAR
SERVICE**

YUROK LOOP TRAIL
False Klamath Cove & Lagoon Creek
1-mile loop, good for kids

TREES OF MYSTERY
Northern CA's best tourism stop
Gondola ride through the canopy

KLAMATH RIVER JET TOURS
2-hour tour with tons of wildlife to see
$45 per adult, $35 teen, $25 per child

KLAMATH RIVER PICNIC AREA
Sweeping views overlooking estuary
Watch for gray whales and seabirds

Requa

RAVENWOOD MOTEL
Perfect base for redwood exploration
$65 - $75 per night

Klamath

LOG CABIN DINER
Great breakfast + burgers & fries
$8 - $12

11) CRESCENT CITY
1 hour 20 minutes Drive Time
60 miles

2 MILES

N

VITA CUCINA BAKERY & FOOD
Diverse menu from pastries to pizza
$2 - $9

TO HOWLAND
HILL ROAD

5TH

Elk

ELK-VALLEY

FRONT

G

D

RUMIANO CHEESE COMPANY
CA's oldest family-owned cheese co.
Sample the smoked mozzarella & more

LIGHTHOUSE INN
Cozy base of operations for CA coast
$90 - $145 per night

P

OCEAN WORLD
Pet a shark and watch the seal show
$13 per adult, $8 per child

CHART ROOM RESTAURANT
Waterside setting with seafood fare
$5 - $28, also $3 wine by the glass

BATTERY POINT LIGHTHOUSE
Scenic lighthouse on sea stack
Visit during low tide only

CRESCENT CITY

NORTHERN CALIFORNIA

The northern California coast is a place of quiet redwood groves, isolated coastline, and great natural wonder. On the Oregon border, Redwoods National & State Parks are home to massive trees stretching over 300 feet into the sky. At the Lost Coast, the highway is forced inland many miles while rugged sand beaches march on along the shore. Further south, the highway meets back up with the ocean along expansive bluff terraces and extended inlets.

Of all the Pacific Coast Highway sections, this is the place to venture further off the main road; go on a hike, explore one of the many scenic byways, and find a quiet place to sleep.

CRESCENT CITY

How to Create a National Park

Redwood, unlike many national parks, has been put together grove by grove over the course of 57 years. Throughout the late 1800s and into the 1900s, the lumber industry had unrestricted access to over 2,000,000 acres of old-growth redwoods. While there was an attempt to begin saving the remaining groves in 1911, nothing began to happen until 1921.

The Save-The-Redwoods League, founded in 1918, began the conservation process with the purchase of the Raynal Bolling Memorial Grove (now in Humboldt Redwoods State Park). The founding of the California State Park system in 1927 created Prairie Creek Redwoods, Del Norte Coast Redwoods, and Jedediah Smith Redwoods.

World War II caused further delays in forming an official national park due to the high demands of lumber. Finally, on October 2nd 1968, the bill for Redwood National Park was signed protecting an additional 100,000 acres of forest. Another 48,000 acres were added in 1978, but most of it had been previously logged.

Throughout coastal California you'll find small patches of protected old-growth redwoods. These groves are a testament to the hard work and dedication groups of conservationists had over a hundred years ago. Without them, it is likely none of these redwood giants would remain.

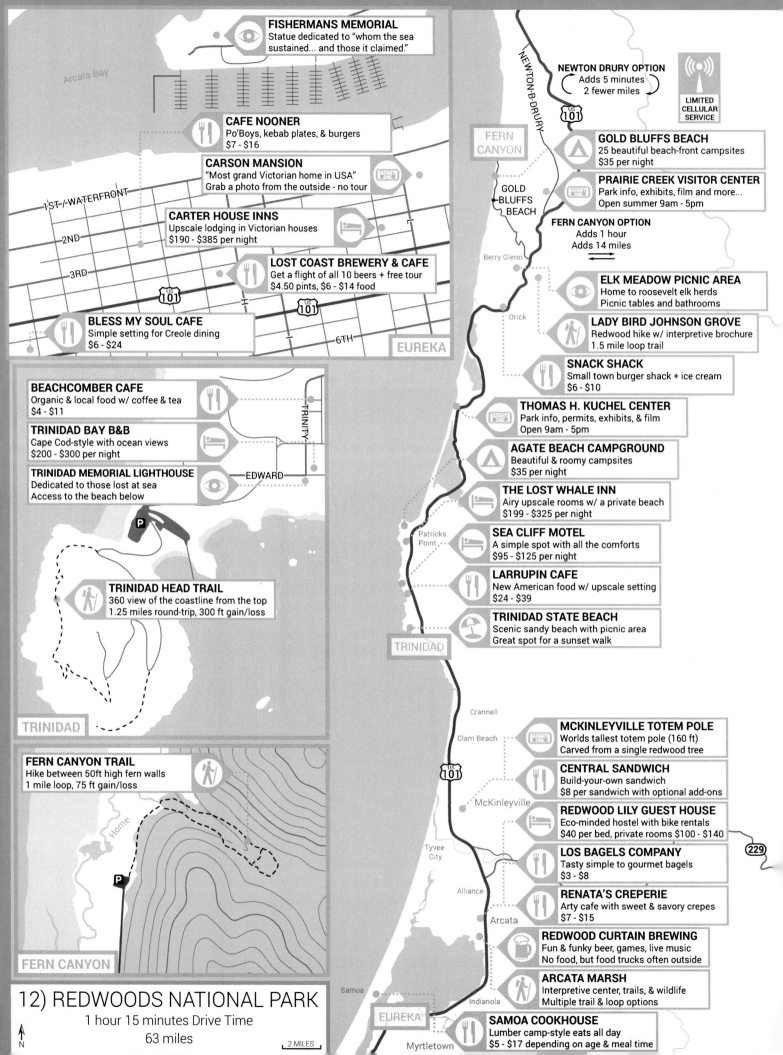

FISHERMANS MEMORIAL
Statue dedicated to "whom the sea sustained... and those it claimed."

Arcata Bay

NEWTON-B-DRURY

NEWTON DRURY OPTION
Adds 5 minutes
2 fewer miles

LIMITED CELLULAR SERVICE

US 101

FERN CANYON

CAFE NOONER
Po'Boys, kebab plates, & burgers
$7 - $16

GOLD BLUFFS BEACH
25 beautiful beach-front campsites
$35 per night

GOLD BLUFFS BEACH

CARSON MANSION
"Most grand Victorian home in USA"
Grab a photo from the outside - no tour

ADMIT ONE

PRAIRIE CREEK VISITOR CENTER
Park info, exhibits, film and more...
Open summer 9am - 5pm

1ST-/WATERFRONT

CARTER HOUSE INNS
Upscale lodging in Victorian houses
$190 - $385 per night

FERN CANYON OPTION
Adds 1 hour
Adds 14 miles

2ND

Berry Glenn

3RD

LOST COAST BREWERY & CAFE
Get a flight of all 10 beers + free tour
$4.50 pints, $6 - $14 food

ELK MEADOW PICNIC AREA
Home to roosevelt elk herds
Picnic tables and bathrooms

US 101

US 101

Orick

LADY BIRD JOHNSON GROVE
Redwood hike w/ interpretive brochure
1.5 mile loop trail

BLESS MY SOUL CAFE
Simple setting for Creole dining
$6 - $24

6TH

EUREKA

SNACK SHACK
Small town burger shack + ice cream
$6 - $10

THOMAS H. KUCHEL CENTER
Park info, permits, exhibits, & film
Open 9am - 5pm

BEACHCOMBER CAFE
Organic & local food w/ coffee & tea
$4 - $11

TRINITY

AGATE BEACH CAMPGROUND
Beautiful & roomy campsites
$35 per night

TRINIDAD BAY B&B
Cape Cod-style with ocean views
$200 - $300 per night

THE LOST WHALE INN
Airy upscale rooms w/ a private beach
$199 - $325 per night

TRINIDAD MEMORIAL LIGHTHOUSE
Dedicated to those lost at sea
Access to the beach below

EDWARD

SEA CLIFF MOTEL
A simple spot with all the comforts
$95 - $125 per night

Patricks Point

P

LARRUPIN CAFE
New American food w/ upscale setting
$24 - $39

TRINIDAD HEAD TRAIL
360 view of the coastline from the top
1.25 miles round-trip, 300 ft gain/loss

TRINIDAD STATE BEACH
Scenic sandy beach with picnic area
Great spot for a sunset walk

TRINIDAD

TRINIDAD

Crannell

MCKINLEYVILLE TOTEM POLE
Worlds tallest totem pole (160 ft)
Carved from a single redwood tree

Clam Beach

FERN CANYON TRAIL
Hike between 50ft high fern walls
1 mile loop, 75 ft gain/loss

CENTRAL SANDWICH
Build-your-own sandwich
$8 per sandwich with optional add-ons

US 101

Home

REDWOOD LILY GUEST HOUSE
Eco-minded hostel with bike rentals
$40 per bed, private rooms $100 - $140

McKinleyville

LOS BAGELS COMPANY
Tasty simple to gourmet bagels
$3 - $8

P

Tyvee City

229

RENATA'S CREPERIE
Arty cafe with sweet & savory crepes
$7 - $15

Alliance

REDWOOD CURTAIN BREWING
Fun & funky beer, games, live music
No food, but food trucks often outside

Arcata

FERN CANYON

ARCATA MARSH
Interpretive center, trails, & wildlife
Multiple trail & loop options

12) REDWOODS NATIONAL PARK
1 hour 15 minutes Drive Time
63 miles

Samoa

EUREKA

Indianola

SAMOA COOKHOUSE
Lumber camp-style eats all day
$5 - $17 depending on age & meal time

N

Myrtletown

2 MILES

REDWOOD NATIONAL PARK

Fun Facts about Redwoods

1) HOW TALL IS TOO TALL?
Coastal redwoods frequently grow to over 300 feet tall. Hyperion, the world's tallest tree on record, stands 379.1 feet tall (that's taller than the Statue of Liberty). Don't bother to go looking for it though -- the location is a fiercely guarded secret.

2) ROOTS FOR DAYS
Redwood roots are shallow, often extending 50 feet out on all sides. This is a good thing, because most redwoods only send their roots down 6 - 12 feet. You can see examples of this intricate root structure while looking at one of these fallen giants.

3) TALL ≠ OLD
A giant sequoia (part of the redwood family), named The President, gets the notoriety of being the fourth oldest living (non-cloning) tree at 3200 years old. However, tucked away along the eastern edge of California lives an even older species - the bristlecone pine. One bristlecone has a verified age of 5065 years old! Other notable stuff from 3000 BC: agriculture began in north Africa, the Sumerians began forming cities, and Troy was founded.

4) CAMEO
Redwood National Park has been the backdrop to many classic films. You might recognize scenes from Star Wars: Return of the Jedi and The Lost World: Jurassic Park, just to name a few. Make sure to watch out for Ewoks and dinosaurs as you explore the park.

5) GOOD THINGS COME IN SMALL PACKAGES
Despite their enormous size, redwoods start off small. A redwood seed is about the same size as a tomato seed (ie: tiny). It would take about 120,000 redwood seeds to equal one pound in weight. It's a good thing that each tree produces about 100,000 seeds each year!

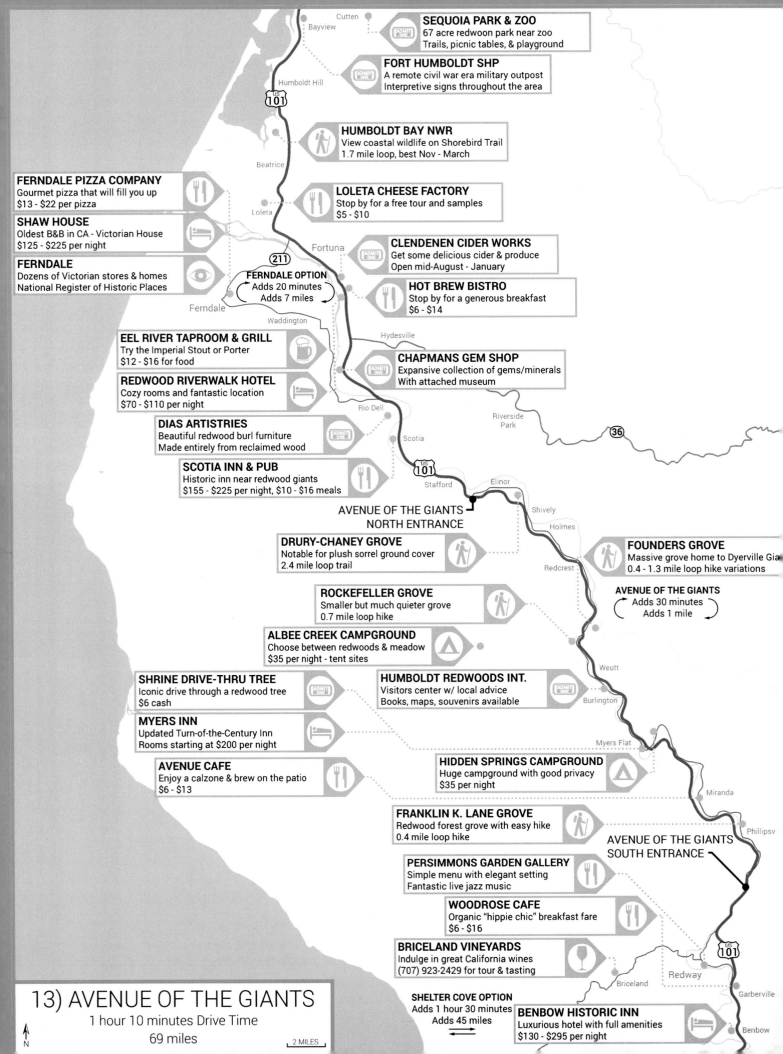

SEQUOIA PARK & ZOO
67 acre redwoon park near zoo
Trails, picnic tables, & playground

FORT HUMBOLDT SHP
A remote civil war era military outpost
Interpretive signs throughout the area

HUMBOLDT BAY NWR
View coastal wildlife on Shorebird Trail
1.7 mile loop, best Nov - March

FERNDALE PIZZA COMPANY
Gourmet pizza that will fill you up
$13 - $22 per pizza

SHAW HOUSE
Oldest B&B in CA - Victorian House
$125 - $225 per night

FERNDALE
Dozens of Victorian stores & homes
National Register of Historic Places

LOLETA CHEESE FACTORY
Stop by for a free tour and samples
$5 - $10

CLENDENEN CIDER WORKS
Get some delicious cider & produce
Open mid-August - January

HOT BREW BISTRO
Stop by for a generous breakfast
$6 - $14

FERNDALE OPTION
Adds 20 minutes
Adds 7 miles

EEL RIVER TAPROOM & GRILL
Try the Imperial Stout or Porter
$12 - $16 for food

REDWOOD RIVERWALK HOTEL
Cozy rooms and fantastic location
$70 - $110 per night

CHAPMANS GEM SHOP
Expansive collection of gems/minerals
With attached museum

DIAS ARTISTRIES
Beautiful redwood burl furniture
Made entirely from reclaimed wood

SCOTIA INN & PUB
Historic inn near redwood giants
$155 - $225 per night, $10 - $16 meals

AVENUE OF THE GIANTS
NORTH ENTRANCE

DRURY-CHANEY GROVE
Notable for plush sorrel ground cover
2.4 mile loop trail

FOUNDERS GROVE
Massive grove home to Dyerville Gia
0.4 - 1.3 mile loop hike variations

AVENUE OF THE GIANTS
Adds 30 minutes
Adds 1 mile

ROCKEFELLER GROVE
Smaller but much quieter grove
0.7 mile loop hike

ALBEE CREEK CAMPGROUND
Choose between redwoods & meadow
$35 per night - tent sites

SHRINE DRIVE-THRU TREE
Iconic drive through a redwood tree
$6 cash

HUMBOLDT REDWOODS INT.
Visitors center w/ local advice
Books, maps, souvenirs available

MYERS INN
Updated Turn-of-the-Century Inn
Rooms starting at $200 per night

AVENUE CAFE
Enjoy a calzone & brew on the patio
$6 - $13

HIDDEN SPRINGS CAMPGROUND
Huge campground with good privacy
$35 per night

FRANKLIN K. LANE GROVE
Redwood forest grove with easy hike
0.4 mile loop hike

AVENUE OF THE GIANTS
SOUTH ENTRANCE

PERSIMMONS GARDEN GALLERY
Simple menu with elegant setting
Fantastic live jazz music

WOODROSE CAFE
Organic "hippie chic" breakfast fare
$6 - $16

BRICELAND VINEYARDS
Indulge in great California wines
(707) 923-2429 for tour & tasting

SHELTER COVE OPTION
Adds 1 hour 30 minutes
Adds 45 miles

BENBOW HISTORIC INN
Luxurious hotel with full amenities
$130 - $295 per night

13) AVENUE OF THE GIANTS
1 hour 10 minutes Drive Time
69 miles

2 MILES

AVENUE OF THE GIANTS

A Place so Good, You Need Two Roads

Avenue of the Giants is a scenic highway extending from Fortuna to Garberville in Humboldt County. This stretch of road used to be part of Highway 101 until a realignment in 1960 created the existing bypass. Now you can appreciate the 50,000+ acres of redwood groves located along this route without the worry of traffic speeding by! It's also the home of the Avenue of the Giants Marathon in early May.

Make sure you don't miss this scenic route -- this is roadside tourism at its best.

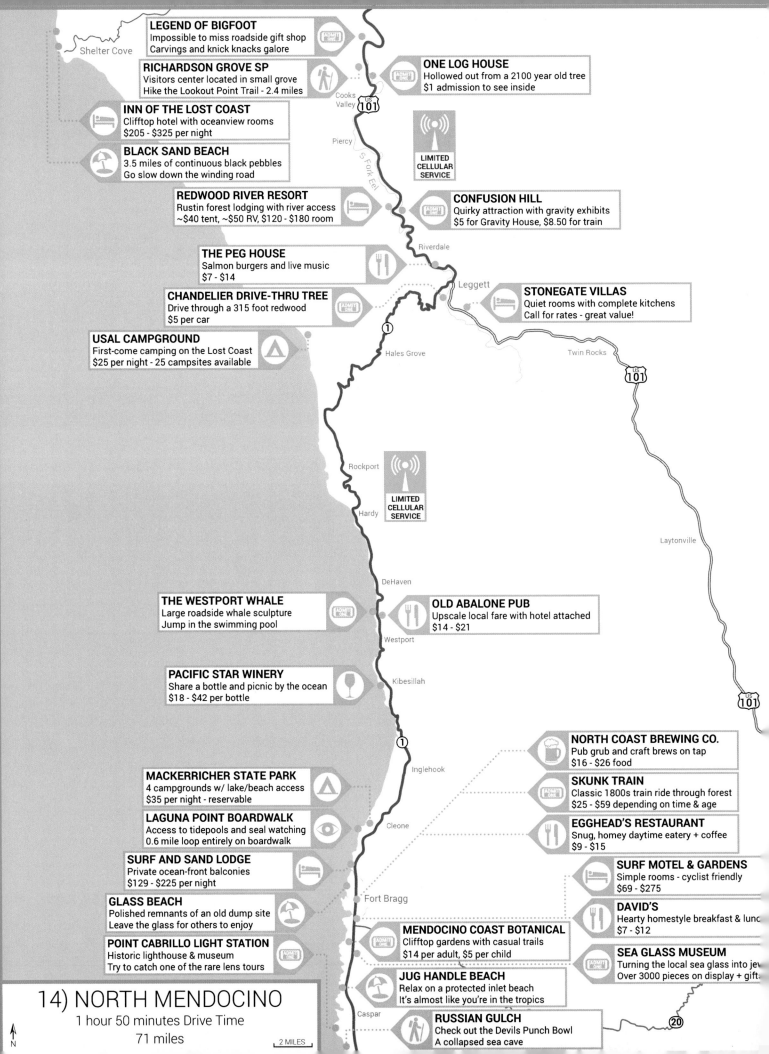

LEGEND OF BIGFOOT
Impossible to miss roadside gift shop
Carvings and knick knacks galore

ONE LOG HOUSE
Hollowed out from a 2100 year old tree
$1 admission to see inside

RICHARDSON GROVE SP
Visitors center located in small grove
Hike the Lookout Point Trail - 2.4 miles

INN OF THE LOST COAST
Clifftop hotel with oceanview rooms
$205 - $325 per night

LIMITED CELLULAR SERVICE

BLACK SAND BEACH
3.5 miles of continuous black pebbles
Go slow down the winding road

REDWOOD RIVER RESORT
Rustin forest lodging with river access
~$40 tent, ~$50 RV, $120 - $180 room

CONFUSION HILL
Quirky attraction with gravity exhibits
$5 for Gravity House, $8.50 for train

THE PEG HOUSE
Salmon burgers and live music
$7 - $14

STONEGATE VILLAS
Quiet rooms with complete kitchens
Call for rates - great value!

CHANDELIER DRIVE-THRU TREE
Drive through a 315 foot redwood
$5 per car

USAL CAMPGROUND
First-come camping on the Lost Coast
$25 per night - 25 campsites available

LIMITED CELLULAR SERVICE

THE WESTPORT WHALE
Large roadside whale sculpture
Jump in the swimming pool

OLD ABALONE PUB
Upscale local fare with hotel attached
$14 - $21

PACIFIC STAR WINERY
Share a bottle and picnic by the ocean
$18 - $42 per bottle

NORTH COAST BREWING CO.
Pub grub and craft brews on tap
$16 - $26 food

MACKERRICHER STATE PARK
4 campgrounds w/ lake/beach access
$35 per night - reservable

SKUNK TRAIN
Classic 1800s train ride through forest
$25 - $59 depending on time & age

LAGUNA POINT BOARDWALK
Access to tidepools and seal watching
0.6 mile loop entirely on boardwalk

EGGHEAD'S RESTAURANT
Snug, homey daytime eatery + coffee
$9 - $15

SURF AND SAND LODGE
Private ocean-front balconies
$129 - $225 per night

SURF MOTEL & GARDENS
Simple rooms - cyclist friendly
$69 - $275

GLASS BEACH
Polished remnants of an old dump site
Leave the glass for others to enjoy

DAVID'S
Hearty homestyle breakfast & lunc
$7 - $12

POINT CABRILLO LIGHT STATION
Historic lighthouse & museum
Try to catch one of the rare lens tours

MENDOCINO COAST BOTANICAL
Clifftop gardens with casual trails
$14 per adult, $5 per child

SEA GLASS MUSEUM
Turning the local sea glass into jew
Over 3000 pieces on display + gifts

JUG HANDLE BEACH
Relax on a protected inlet beach
It's almost like you're in the tropics

14) NORTH MENDOCINO
1 hour 50 minutes Drive Time
71 miles

RUSSIAN GULCH
Check out the Devils Punch Bowl
A collapsed sea cave

2 MILES

N

NORTH MENDOCINO

A Road by Many Names

Highway 1 was put together piece by piece over the course of 40 years. It begins in Leggett, CA to the north and runs all the way down the California coast to Dana Point, CA in the south. Due to so much time elapsing throughout its construction, and also because it is a collection of many smaller roads, it is referred to by many different names.

The California Highway 1 designation was assigned to the complete route, all the way up to Rockport, in 1964. Various stretches of the highway have additional names such as Pacific Coast Highway from Dana Point to Santa Barbara, Cabrillo Highway from Santa Barbara to San Francisco, and Shoreline Highway from San Francisco to Leggett. To muddle the matter further, sections of Highway 1 and Highway 101 are combined for long stretches, most notable from Ventura through Gaviota.

Initially, there were plans to extend Highway 1 north from Rockport to Ferndale. However, in 1984 those plans were dismissed due to the challenges and costs associated with building through the coastal mountains of the Lost Coast. Instead, Highway 208 from Rockport to Leggett was redesignated as the final piece to Highway 1, which now extends to its terminus along Highway 101.

So the iconic scenery along Big Sur is actually NOT found along the Pacific Coast Highway, but is found along the Cabrillo Highway. Fun facts to know and share!

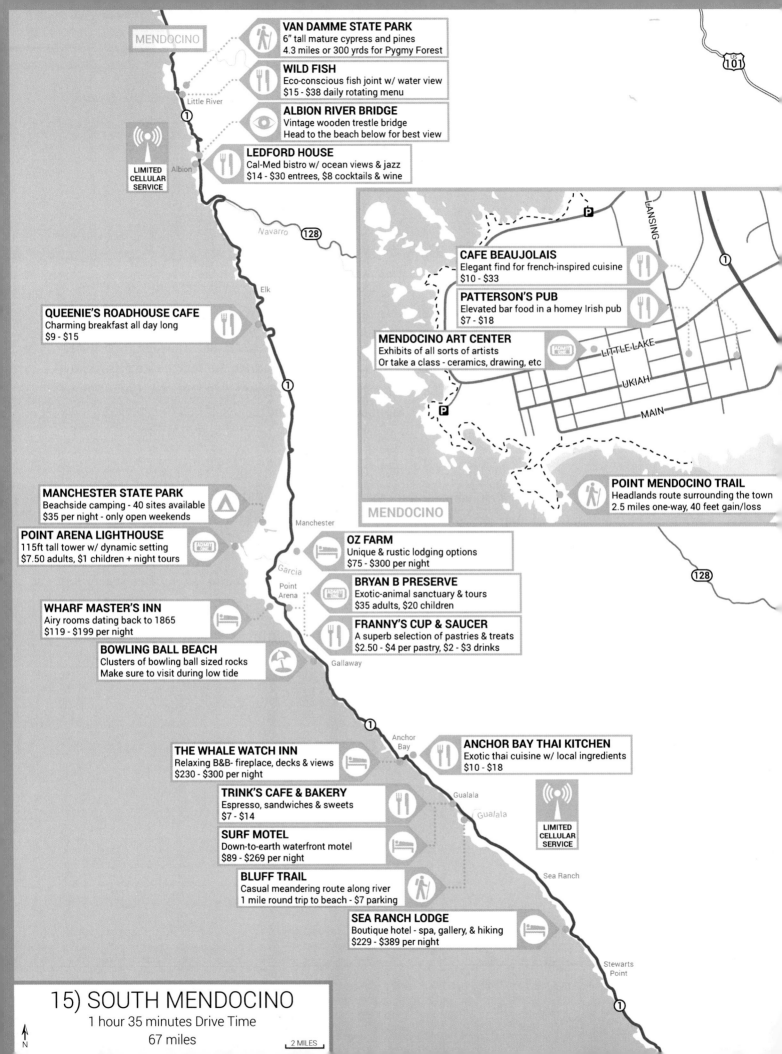

VAN DAMME STATE PARK
6" tall mature cypress and pines
4.3 miles or 300 yrds for Pygmy Forest

WILD FISH
Eco-conscious fish joint w/ water view
$15 - $38 daily rotating menu

ALBION RIVER BRIDGE
Vintage wooden trestle bridge
Head to the beach below for best view

LEDFORD HOUSE
Cal-Med bistro w/ ocean views & jazz
$14 - $30 entrees, $8 cocktails & wine

LIMITED CELLULAR SERVICE

CAFE BEAUJOLAIS
Elegant find for french-inspired cuisine
$10 - $33

PATTERSON'S PUB
Elevated bar food in a homey Irish pub
$7 - $18

MENDOCINO ART CENTER
Exhibits of all sorts of artists
Or take a class - ceramics, drawing, etc

QUEENIE'S ROADHOUSE CAFE
Charming breakfast all day long
$9 - $15

POINT MENDOCINO TRAIL
Headlands route surrounding the town
2.5 miles one-way, 40 feet gain/loss

MENDOCINO

MANCHESTER STATE PARK
Beachside camping - 40 sites available
$35 per night - only open weekends

POINT ARENA LIGHTHOUSE
115ft tall tower w/ dynamic setting
$7.50 adults, $1 children + night tours

OZ FARM
Unique & rustic lodging options
$75 - $300 per night

BRYAN B PRESERVE
Exotic-animal sanctuary & tours
$35 adults, $20 children

WHARF MASTER'S INN
Airy rooms dating back to 1865
$119 - $199 per night

FRANNY'S CUP & SAUCER
A superb selection of pastries & treats
$2.50 - $4 per pastry, $2 - $3 drinks

BOWLING BALL BEACH
Clusters of bowling ball sized rocks
Make sure to visit during low tide

THE WHALE WATCH INN
Relaxing B&B- fireplace, decks & views
$230 - $300 per night

ANCHOR BAY THAI KITCHEN
Exotic thai cuisine w/ local ingredients
$10 - $18

TRINK'S CAFE & BAKERY
Espresso, sandwiches & sweets
$7 - $14

LIMITED CELLULAR SERVICE

SURF MOTEL
Down-to-earth waterfront motel
$89 - $269 per night

BLUFF TRAIL
Casual meandering route along river
1 mile round trip to beach - $7 parking

SEA RANCH LODGE
Boutique hotel - spa, gallery, & hiking
$229 - $389 per night

15) SOUTH MENDOCINO
1 hour 35 minutes Drive Time
67 miles

2 MILES

N

SOUTH MENDOCINO

5-Night Northern California Camping Itinerary: Local Advice from Hipcamp

It's hard to find roads to watch whales from these days; no one seems to be working on a bridge to Hawaii, and there haven't been any encouraging attempts to put I-5 in a gigantic aquarium tube either. Thankfully, though, CA-1 exists. To help you get in on the greatest road in the greatest state, we put together a camping itinerary for a 5-day trip up to the Oregon border from SF.

CHANSLOR RANCH
A 378-acre horse ranch with approximately one-zillion campsites, Chanslor Ranch has a diversity of places to set up camp that range from exposed ocean views to wooded streamside retreats. Their group sites make it easy to bring all your friends as well!

ROSEMAN CREEK RANCH
A cob sleeping cabin and an outdoor shower make this redwood hideaway spectacular in a "maybe I was meant to be a mythical forest gnome" kind of way. Complete with beautiful kitchen garden and brick oven, it's hard to compete with Roseman Creek's #homesteadgoals.

MACKERRICHER STATE PARK
Through you'll have to make reservations outside of Hipcamp, camping at MacKerricher is worth the hassle. 9 miles of beaches, loads of trails, and a beach with a famously confounding accumulation of sea glass make Mac-K one of the gems of California's park system!

USAL BEACH CAMP
The only drive-in campsite in the Sinkyone Wilderness, Usal Beach Camp is both accessible and out-there. It is also the southern terminus for the lost coast trail, so if you'd like to amend your itinerary to include a backpacking trip, this is where you'd park anyway. Reservations (and permits for backpacking) are through the CA state parks.

OTTER SPACE
Typo dolphinitely intended, Otter Space is an off-the-grid retreat and healing center, complete with redwoods, meadows, and waterfont on the mighty Klamath River. Set up in the meadow or rent a tee-pee, yurt, or cabin for a blissful night on your CA-1 roadtrip!

Hipcamp is the best way to discover and book your next camping trip. Search over 280,000 campsites across the US. From public parks to private land, we're the most comprehensive guide to camping across the country.

PYGMY FOREST
Mature but stunted forests & prairie
3.8 mile loop

OCEAN COVE BAR & GRILL
Beer battered cod, salmon & prawn
$10 - $16

FORT ROSS STATE HIST. PARK
Russian-era fort compound
$8 per car, open daily 10am - 4:30pm

FORT ROSS VINEYARD
Tasting room with panoramic views
$45 - $70 per bottle

RIVER'S END RESTAURANT
3 course eatery with sunset views
~$60 for 3 course meal, ~$30 entrees

ALAMERE FALLS - PALOMARIN
Waterfall onto a beach? I think I will...
8.3 miles or 14 miles via Wildcat Camp

ALAMERE FALLS

MESA

ALAMERE FALLS

GOAT ROCK STATE BEACH
Long sandy beaches & craggy bluffs
Stop and stretch your legs

WRIGHT'S BEACH
Beach camping at its best!
$35 tent/RV, $7 hiker/biker, $8 day-use

PORTUGUESE BEACH
Scenic, sandy beach w/ rocky bluffs
Popular rock & surf fishing spot

ARCHED ROCK VIEWPOINT
Pullout on coastal side of the road
Monolithic rock arch in the water

BODEGA DUNES CAMPGROUND
Secluded campsites near the beach
$35 per night, $6 for hiker/biker sites

TERRAPIN CREEK CAFE
Relaxed spot for eclectic world cuisine
$15 starters, $26 - $36 entrees

BODEGA HARBOR INN
Rooms w/ woodstoves on the harbor
$80 - $155 per night

FISHERMAN'S COVE
Seafood shack with delicious variety
$8 - $15, $22 for a dozen raw oysters

POTTER SCHOOL HOUSE
Famous filming location of
Alfred Hitchcock's "The Birds"

ESTERO CAFE
Locally sourced breakfast & brunch
$7 - $16

TOMALES BAKERY
Sweet & savory treats everyone loves
$3 pastries & breads

NICK'S COVE
Seafood spot w/ fishing lodge feel
$9 - $26, $3.25 raw oysters

HOG ISLAND OYSTER CO.
Reserve ahead for a Shuck-Your-Own
picnic or a seat at The Boat Oyster Bar

BLUE WATERS KAYAKING
Hourly or overnight rentals + tours
$50 for 2 hours, $100 for overnight

MILLERTON POINT
Dramatic views of Tomales Bay
Easy loop hike - dog friendly

COWGIRL CREAMERY
Reserve a tasting time ($5)
Or take a cheese making 101 class

POINT REYES SHIPWRECKS
Picturesque beached shipwreck
Trail behind the grocery store

MOTEL INVERNESS
Relaxed rooms + a meditation garden
$145 - $325 per night

ABBOTTS LAGOON TRAIL
Quiet hike past lagoon to long beach
2.8 miles + more beach walking

CYPRESS TREE TUNNEL
Beautiful trees and a radio station
Visit at sunset for the best light

BEAR VALLEY VISITORS CENTER
Exhibits, permits, park movie, & shop
Open 10am - 5pm

POINT REYES LIGHTHOUSE
Visitors center, exhibits, and history
Follow the stairs down to thlens room

CHIMNEY ROCK TRAIL
Views of Drakes Bay & Pacific Ocean
1.6 miles out-and-back

POINT REYES OPTION
Adds 35 minutes
Adds 20 miles

FIVE BROOKS RANCH
Trail & beach horseback riding
$40 - $180 depending on length

ALAMERE FALLS

THE SIREN CANTEEN
Beachside location & summer fare
Lemonade, margaritas, & fries ~$10

STEEP RAVINE CAMPGROUND
Primitive camping on ocean bluffs
$25 tent sites, $100 cabins

16) POINT REYES SEASHORE
2 hours 20 minutes Drive Time
81 miles

2 MILES

N

POINT REYES SEASHORE

A Little Bit about Tomales Bay

Thirty-five miles northwest of San Francisco sits Tomales Bay, a straight-and-narrow inlet extending fifteen miles long. Tomales Bay is a fascinating geologic spot where rocks from the Tehachapi Mountains, a range located 310 miles to the south, are strangely found.

Here's how it happened.

If you were to draw a line down the middle of Tomales Bay, you'd find the exact location of the San Andreas Fault as it extends north from San Francisco. The west side of the bay is the eastern edge of the Pacific Tectonic Plate, while the eastern side of the bay is the western edge of the North American Tectonic Plate. The San Andreas Fault is a great example of a transform fault. Picture two cars passing each other on a two-way street -- that's exactly what's happening here, except those cars are moving at the same rate that your fingernails grow. The movement isn't a continuous affair, instead the tension builds up over many years until the plates slip, causing an earthquake. Point Reyes will continue to move northward, so catch it while you can!

Do you know what else Tomales Bay is great for?

Oysters!

Stop by Tomales Bay Oyster Company or Hog Island Oyster Company, bring a picnic, and enjoy bivalves straight out of the water!

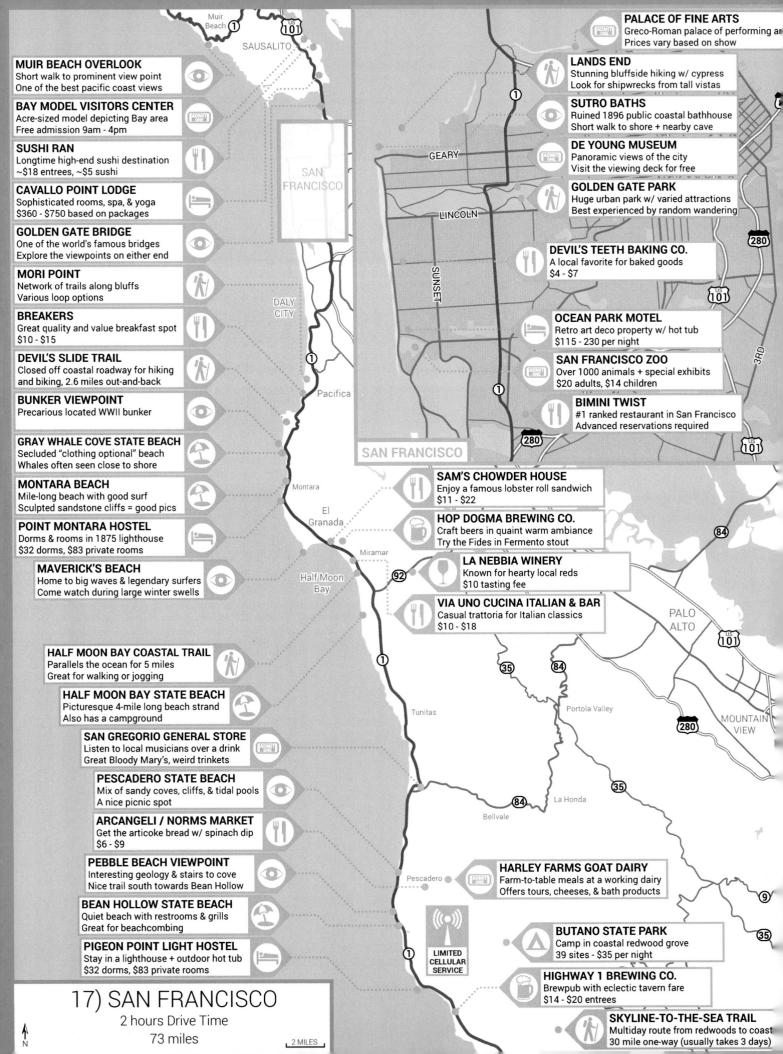

PALACE OF FINE ARTS
Greco-Roman palace of performing ar
Prices vary based on show

MUIR BEACH OVERLOOK
Short walk to prominent view point
One of the best pacific coast views

BAY MODEL VISITORS CENTER
Acre-sized model depicting Bay area
Free admission 9am - 4pm

SUSHI RAN
Longtime high-end sushi destination
~$18 entrees, ~$5 sushi

CAVALLO POINT LODGE
Sophisticated rooms, spa, & yoga
$360 - $750 based on packages

GOLDEN GATE BRIDGE
One of the world's famous bridges
Explore the viewpoints on either end

MORI POINT
Network of trails along bluffs
Various loop options

BREAKERS
Great quality and value breakfast spot
$10 - $15

DEVIL'S SLIDE TRAIL
Closed off coastal roadway for hiking
and biking, 2.6 miles out-and-back

BUNKER VIEWPOINT
Precarious located WWII bunker

GRAY WHALE COVE STATE BEACH
Secluded "clothing optional" beach
Whales often seen close to shore

MONTARA BEACH
Mile-long beach with good surf
Sculpted sandstone cliffs = good pics

POINT MONTARA HOSTEL
Dorms & rooms in 1875 lighthouse
$32 dorms, $83 private rooms

MAVERICK'S BEACH
Home to big waves & legendary surfers
Come watch during large winter swells

HALF MOON BAY COASTAL TRAIL
Parallels the ocean for 5 miles
Great for walking or jogging

HALF MOON BAY STATE BEACH
Picturesque 4-mile long beach strand
Also has a campground

SAN GREGORIO GENERAL STORE
Listen to local musicians over a drink
Great Bloody Mary's, weird trinkets

PESCADERO STATE BEACH
Mix of sandy coves, cliffs, & tidal pools
A nice picnic spot

ARCANGELI / NORMS MARKET
Get the articoke bread w/ spinach dip
$6 - $9

PEBBLE BEACH VIEWPOINT
Interesting geology & stairs to cove
Nice trail south towards Bean Hollow

BEAN HOLLOW STATE BEACH
Quiet beach with restrooms & grills
Great for beachcombing

PIGEON POINT LIGHT HOSTEL
Stay in a lighthouse + outdoor hot tub
$32 dorms, $83 private rooms

LANDS END
Stunning bluffside hiking w/ cypress
Look for shipwrecks from tall vistas

SUTRO BATHS
Ruined 1896 public coastal bathhouse
Short walk to shore + nearby cave

DE YOUNG MUSEUM
Panoramic views of the city
Visit the viewing deck for free

GOLDEN GATE PARK
Huge urban park w/ varied attractions
Best experienced by random wandering

DEVIL'S TEETH BAKING CO.
A local favorite for baked goods
$4 - $7

OCEAN PARK MOTEL
Retro art deco property w/ hot tub
$115 - 230 per night

SAN FRANCISCO ZOO
Over 1000 animals + special exhibits
$20 adults, $14 children

BIMINI TWIST
#1 ranked restaurant in San Francisco
Advanced reservations required

SAM'S CHOWDER HOUSE
Enjoy a famous lobster roll sandwich
$11 - $22

HOP DOGMA BREWING CO.
Craft beers in quaint warm ambiance
Try the Fides in Fermento stout

LA NEBBIA WINERY
Known for hearty local reds
$10 tasting fee

VIA UNO CUCINA ITALIAN & BAR
Casual trattoria for Italian classics
$10 - $18

HARLEY FARMS GOAT DAIRY
Farm-to-table meals at a working dairy
Offers tours, cheeses, & bath products

BUTANO STATE PARK
Camp in coastal redwood grove
39 sites - $35 per night

HIGHWAY 1 BREWING CO.
Brewpub with eclectic tavern fare
$14 - $20 entrees

SKYLINE-TO-THE-SEA TRAIL
Multiday route from redwoods to coast
30 mile one-way (usually takes 3 days)

LIMITED CELLULAR SERVICE

17) SAN FRANCISCO
2 hours Drive Time
73 miles

2 MILES

N

CENTRAL COAST

The central coast portion of Highway 1 has a little bit of everything. At its northern boundary, San Francisco provides a plethora of urban eateries and attractions. Highway 1 then follows the coast past Half Moon Bay, where you can find quiet beaches and long stretches of open road reminiscent of northern California. At Monterey and Santa Cruz you'll find luxurious hotels, amazing breweries and wineries, and plenty of opportunities for hiking, kayaking, and surfing.

South of Carmel-By-The-Sea, the mountain encroaches on the ocean along the stunning Big Sur section, arguably the most scenic part of the entire pacific coast. Wildlife abounds south of Big Sur at the elephant seal rookery of San Simeon and pristine estuary of Morro Bay. Finally, the highway heads inland around Point Conception until it reaches the Santa Barbara Channel.

If you only have time to drive one section of the pacific coast, I would make the Central Coast the one.

SAN FRANCISCO

4 Must-See Stops Along Big Sur: Local Advice from Dylan Gallagher

Castroville Fruit Stands are a great spot to pick up fresh, local-grown produce before you enter the Big Sur region. You can avoid the higher-than-normal price tags of Big Sur, and find some great deals in the process (5 avocados for $1).

Andrew Molera State Park is a walk-in only campground located at the mouth of the Big Sur River. You can hike, fish or surf, all within walking distance of your campsite. The campground is first-come, first-serve only, though, so show up early to grab your spot.

Bixby Bridge is a landmark most people associate with Big Sur. Pull over on the side of the road for a selfie with the turquoise water, rugged California cliffs and aesthetically-pleasing bridge behind you.

Pfeiffer Beach, known for its purple sand and iconic rock formations (great to include in your sunset photos), is a small beach 2 miles south of Big Sur Lodge. You can find the access road marked by the sign "Narrow Road." A $10 parking fee is required.

Dylan Gallagher operates Orange Sky Adventures, a travel company based in San Francisco, CA. They offer Trips + Treks + Tours of California and beyond. For more information, please visit www.OrangeSkyCo.com or follow him on Instagram @ OrangeSkyCo.

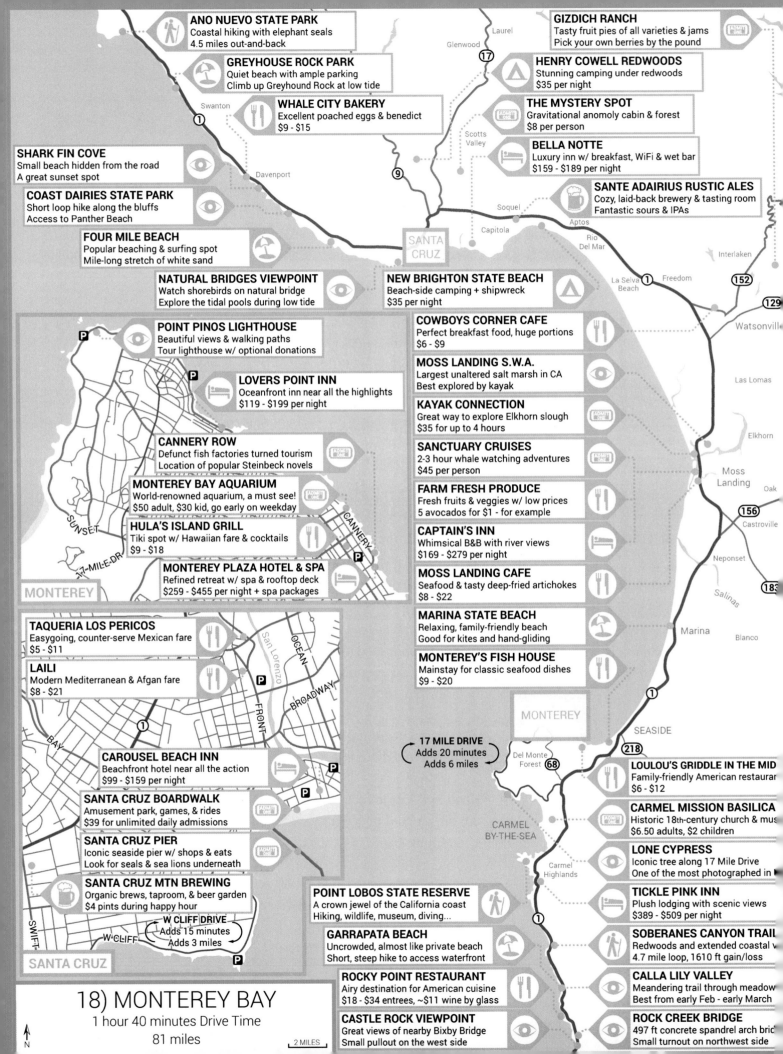

ANO NUEVO STATE PARK
Coastal hiking with elephant seals
4.5 miles out-and-back

GREYHOUSE ROCK PARK
Quiet beach with ample parking
Climb up Greyhound Rock at low tide

WHALE CITY BAKERY
Excellent poached eggs & benedict
$9 - $15

SHARK FIN COVE
Small beach hidden from the road
A great sunset spot

COAST DAIRIES STATE PARK
Short loop hike along the bluffs
Access to Panther Beach

FOUR MILE BEACH
Popular beaching & surfing spot
Mile-long stretch of white sand

NATURAL BRIDGES VIEWPOINT
Watch shorebirds on natural bridge
Explore the tidal pools during low tide

POINT PINOS LIGHTHOUSE
Beautiful views & walking paths
Tour lighthouse w/ optional donations

LOVERS POINT INN
Oceanfront inn near all the highlights
$119 - $199 per night

CANNERY ROW
Defunct fish factories turned tourism
Location of popular Steinbeck novels

MONTEREY BAY AQUARIUM
World-renowned aquarium, a must see!
$50 adult, $30 kid, go early on weekday

HULA'S ISLAND GRILL
Tiki spot w/ Hawaiian fare & cocktails
$9 - $18

MONTEREY PLAZA HOTEL & SPA
Refined retreat w/ spa & rooftop deck
$259 - $455 per night + spa packages

TAQUERIA LOS PERICOS
Easygoing, counter-serve Mexican fare
$5 - $11

LAILI
Modern Mediterranean & Afgan fare
$8 - $21

CAROUSEL BEACH INN
Beachfront hotel near all the action
$99 - $159 per night

SANTA CRUZ BOARDWALK
Amusement park, games, & rides
$39 for unlimited daily admissions

SANTA CRUZ PIER
Iconic seaside pier w/ shops & eats
Look for seals & sea lions underneath

SANTA CRUZ MTN BREWING
Organic brews, taproom, & beer garden
$4 pints during happy hour

W CLIFF DRIVE
Adds 15 minutes
Adds 3 miles

18) MONTEREY BAY
1 hour 40 minutes Drive Time
81 miles

2 MILES

GIZDICH RANCH
Tasty fruit pies of all varieties & jams
Pick your own berries by the pound

HENRY COWELL REDWOODS
Stunning camping under redwoods
$35 per night

THE MYSTERY SPOT
Gravitational anomaly cabin & forest
$8 per person

BELLA NOTTE
Luxury inn w/ breakfast, WiFi & wet bar
$159 - $189 per night

SANTE ADAIRIUS RUSTIC ALES
Cozy, laid-back brewery & tasting room
Fantastic sours & IPAs

NEW BRIGHTON STATE BEACH
Beach-side camping + shipwreck
$35 per night

COWBOYS CORNER CAFE
Perfect breakfast food, huge portions
$6 - $9

MOSS LANDING S.W.A.
Largest unaltered salt marsh in CA
Best explored by kayak

KAYAK CONNECTION
Great way to explore Elkhorn slough
$35 for up to 4 hours

SANCTUARY CRUISES
2-3 hour whale watching adventures
$45 per person

FARM FRESH PRODUCE
Fresh fruits & veggies w/ low prices
5 avocados for $1 - for example

CAPTAIN'S INN
Whimsical B&B with river views
$169 - $279 per night

MOSS LANDING CAFE
Seafood & tasty deep-fried artichokes
$8 - $22

MARINA STATE BEACH
Relaxing, family-friendly beach
Good for kites and hand-gliding

MONTEREY'S FISH HOUSE
Mainstay for classic seafood dishes
$9 - $20

17 MILE DRIVE
Adds 20 minutes
Adds 6 miles

LOULOU'S GRIDDLE IN THE MID
Family-friendly American restaurar
$6 - $12

CARMEL MISSION BASILICA
Historic 18th-century church & mus
$6.50 adults, $2 children

LONE CYPRESS
Iconic tree along 17 Mile Drive
One of the most photographed in

TICKLE PINK INN
Plush lodging with scenic views
$389 - $509 per night

SOBERANES CANYON TRAIL
Redwoods and extended coastal v
4.7 mile loop, 1610 ft gain/loss

CALLA LILY VALLEY
Meandering trail through meadow
Best from early Feb - early March

ROCK CREEK BRIDGE
497 ft concrete spandrel arch brid
Small turnout on northwest side

POINT LOBOS STATE RESERVE
A crown jewel of the California coast
Hiking, wildlife, museum, diving...

GARRAPATA BEACH
Uncrowded, almost like private beach
Short, steep hike to access waterfront

ROCKY POINT RESTAURANT
Airy destination for American cuisine
$18 - $34 entrees, ~$11 wine by glass

CASTLE ROCK VIEWPOINT
Great views of nearby Bixby Bridge
Small pullout on the west side

MONTEREY BAY

Favorite Spots along the Central Coast: Local Advice from Josh McNair

DEVILS SLIDE TRAIL
The Devil's Slide area of Pacific Coast Highway used to be an actual part of the road that was rather dangerous for drivers. They have since moved the road into a tunnel that is much safer and have opened the old Devil's Slide as a biking / hiking path. It is a beautiful spot to get out and enjoy views of the coast while being active.

SAM'S CHOWDER HOUSE
Located in Half Moon Bay, Sam's Chowder House is one of the most popular stops for food along the drive and it is pretty much always crowded. The go to item is the lobster roll which has been on a few "best sandwiches in America" lists. The restaurant overlooks the water and it's a great spot for a nice meal.

NATURAL BRIDGES STATE PARK
This state park, located in the North part of Santa Cruz is a beautiful spot to just sit and enjoy the beach. The highlight though is the massive rock arch that stands about 20 feet out in the water. The park is called bridges because there used to be two but since the other one collapsed it is just the one main arch out in the water.

McWAY FALLS
One of the most iconic stops on the entire drive is the beautiful McWay Waterfall that cascades directly onto the beach. This is an easy 5-minute hike that leads to the overlook for the waterfall. No trip down PCH is complete without taking a few minutes to observe it.

SPLASH CAFE
Probably my favorite meal on PCH is the clam chowder in a bread bowl from Splash Cafe. This decadent soup never ceases to amaze me, and it is easily the best clam chowder I have had. The actual restaurant in Pismo Beach is a fun historic spot as well, and you can take your soup to go and eat it on the beach if you would like.

Josh McNair is the creator of CaliforniaThroughMyLens.com, a website that is dedicated to exploring and cataloging the beauty of California. Everything from restaurants and hikes to road trips and strange attractions are explored on the site. Check it out for even more great ideas to explore the pacific coast.

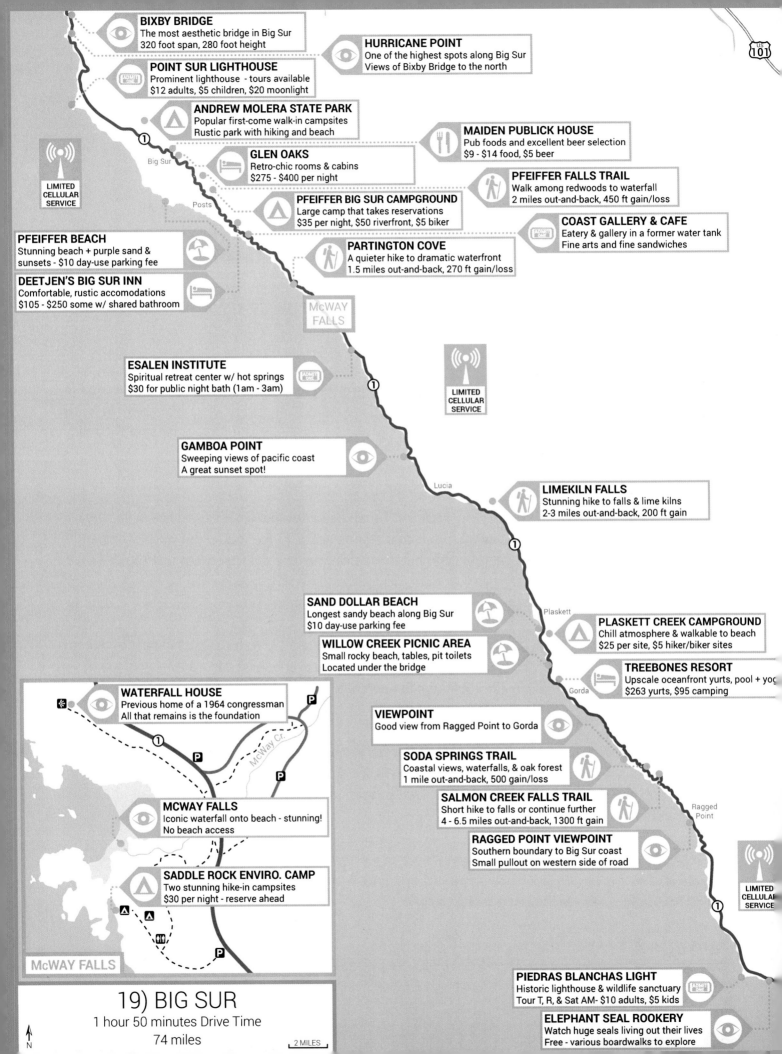

BIXBY BRIDGE
The most aesthetic bridge in Big Sur
320 foot span, 280 foot height

HURRICANE POINT
One of the highest spots along Big Sur
Views of Bixby Bridge to the north

POINT SUR LIGHTHOUSE
Prominent lighthouse - tours available
$12 adults, $5 children, $20 moonlight

ANDREW MOLERA STATE PARK
Popular first-come walk-in campsites
Rustic park with hiking and beach

MAIDEN PUBLICK HOUSE
Pub foods and excellent beer selection
$9 - $14 food, $5 beer

GLEN OAKS
Retro-chic rooms & cabins
$275 - $400 per night

PFEIFFER FALLS TRAIL
Walk among redwoods to waterfall
2 miles out-and-back, 450 ft gain/loss

PFEIFFER BIG SUR CAMPGROUND
Large camp that takes reservations
$35 per night, $50 riverfront, $5 biker

COAST GALLERY & CAFE
Eatery & gallery in a former water tank
Fine arts and fine sandwiches

PFEIFFER BEACH
Stunning beach + purple sand &
sunsets - $10 day-use parking fee

PARTINGTON COVE
A quieter hike to dramatic waterfront
1.5 miles out-and-back, 270 ft gain/loss

DEETJEN'S BIG SUR INN
Comfortable, rustic accomodations
$105 - $250 some w/ shared bathroom

ESALEN INSTITUTE
Spiritual retreat center w/ hot springs
$30 for public night bath (1am - 3am)

GAMBOA POINT
Sweeping views of pacific coast
A great sunset spot!

LIMEKILN FALLS
Stunning hike to falls & lime kilns
2-3 miles out-and-back, 200 ft gain

SAND DOLLAR BEACH
Longest sandy beach along Big Sur
$10 day-use parking fee

PLASKETT CREEK CAMPGROUND
Chill atmosphere & walkable to beach
$25 per site, $5 hiker/biker sites

WILLOW CREEK PICNIC AREA
Small rocky beach, tables, pit toilets
Located under the bridge

TREEBONES RESORT
Upscale oceanfront yurts, pool + yog
$263 yurts, $95 camping

WATERFALL HOUSE
Previous home of a 1964 congressman
All that remains is the foundation

VIEWPOINT
Good view from Ragged Point to Gorda

SODA SPRINGS TRAIL
Coastal views, waterfalls, & oak forest
1 mile out-and-back, 500 gain/loss

SALMON CREEK FALLS TRAIL
Short hike to falls or continue further
4 - 6.5 miles out-and-back, 1300 ft gain

MCWAY FALLS
Iconic waterfall onto beach - stunning!
No beach access

RAGGED POINT VIEWPOINT
Southern boundary to Big Sur coast
Small pullout on western side of road

SADDLE ROCK ENVIRO. CAMP
Two stunning hike-in campsites
$30 per night - reserve ahead

PIEDRAS BLANCHAS LIGHT
Historic lighthouse & wildlife sanctuary
Tour T, R, & Sat AM- $10 adults, $5 kids

19) BIG SUR
1 hour 50 minutes Drive Time
74 miles

ELEPHANT SEAL ROOKERY
Watch huge seals living out their lives
Free - various boardwalks to explore

LIMITED CELLULAR SERVICE

McWAY FALLS

2 MILES

BIG SUR

Tips for Driving Safely along Big Sur

Slow Down - This is a scenic drive that is best appreciated at a slow pace with frequent stops. If you're in a hurry, then heading over to I-5 is your best bet. Don't make a tour reservation at Hearst Castle with the misconception that driving down Big Sur is only going to take an hour or two.

Be a Driver, not a Sightseer - When you're behind the wheel, that's the only thing you get to do. That means no looking at your phone (there isn't service here anyway), no fiddling with the music (that's your co-pilot's job), and no looking at the beautiful scenery. There are plenty of opportunities to pull over and take a look (and switch drivers!), so take advantage of them.

Plan on Driving Defensively - Just because you are an awesome driver doesn't mean that the folks you're sharing the road with are. Practice good defensive driving and give yourself plenty of space.

Wait Out Bad Weather - There's no reason to drive along Big Sur in heavy rain and fog. You're going for the views, so find a nice cafe and relax while the weather rolls over -- it doesn't usually last very long.

Pull Over if You're Going Slowly - It's actually a state law that you must let cars behind you pass if there's a line of 5 or more vehicles. Getting rid of the tailgaters is a great way to stay relaxed while on the road.

Wait to Pass - If you're behind a slow driver, just relax and wait for an opportunity to pass. There are very few places to safely pass along this stretch of road, so wait until they pull over to let you go. If they don't, a good option is for YOU to pull over, take a look at a nice viewpoint, and get going after there is some distance between you two.

Give Advanced Warning when you Stop - Turn on your signal 100 yards in advance to help everyone behind you know what you're planning to do. When you pull off the road, make sure your vehicle is all the way off of the road.

Have a Plan - Sure, if you see something awesome then by all means be impulsive and check it out. But having an overall plan of where you want to stop will help keep you on track and prevent you from missing anything.

HEARST CASTLE
Lavish hilltop castle of a media genius
Tour for $25 per person

SEBASTIAN'S
Burger & wine bar with ocean views
$6 - $11, the burgers here are the best!

SAND PEBBLES INN
Oceanfront rooms with fireplaces
$199 - $299 per night

MOONSTONE BEACH
Enjoy a sunset stroll on the boardwalk
Beachcomb for beautiful pebbles

CUTRUZZOLA VINEYARDS
Boutique winery with intimate setting
Try the Pinot Noir & Reisling

ROBIN'S RESTAURANT
Global fare w/ great vegetarian options
$12 - $24, good happy hour (3-5pm)

MORRO ROCK
Iconic monolith surrounded by ocean
Look for peregrine falcons & sea otters

THE GALLEY SEAFOOD GRILL
Sit down seafood with a beautiful view
$20 - $30 entrees

SHINE CAFE
Vegetarian/Vegan cafe + juice bar
$5 - $10

456 EMBARCADERO INN
Waterfront hotel on Morro Bay estuary
$129 - $229 per night

MORRO BAY STATE PARK
Situated right across from the estuary
$35 per night

MUSEUM OF NATURAL HISTORY
Interactive exhibits of central coast
Donations accepted

KAYAK SHACK
Explore the estuary & dunes via boat
$14 singles, $18 doubles, $18 SUP

RUDDELL'S SMOKEHOUSE
Amazing smoked salmon tacos
$6 per taco

BROWN BUTTER COOKIE CO.
Freshly baked and full of flavor
$1 per cookie

SEASIDE MOTEL
Laid-back lodging w/ a quirky garden
$90 - $150 per night, various rooms

MORRO STRAND STATE BEACH
3-mile sandy beach perfect for walks
Easy parking + toilets at Morro Rock

BLACK HILL TRAIL
For the best aerial view of the bay
1.9 miles out-and-back, 625 ft gain

BISHOP PEAK TRAIL
Hike the tallest of the Nine Sisters
3.5 miles out-and-back, 950 ft gain

FIRESTONE GRILL
BBQ. Get the tri-tip sandwich
$8 - $14

MADONNA INN
Beautiful & whimsical getaway spot
$200 - $300 per night

ISLAY CREEK CAMPGROUND
ENV site 3 for privacy and view (below)
$25 per night

BLUFF TRAIL
Visit the Corallina Cove tidal pools
1 to 3.5 miles loop, mostly flat

AVILA BEACH
Classy and sheltered town beach
Great shopping and food blocks away

SYCAMORE MINERAL SPRIN
Historic mineral spring resort
$40 for a hot tub and bottle of wine

OLD WEST CINNAMON ROLLS
8 different kinds of rolls + coffee
$2 - $3 per roll

SPLASH CAFE
Get the bread bowl clam chowder
$7 per bowl

MON AMI CREPERIE CAFE
Cozy cafe w/amazing crepes & panini
$7 - $10

BUTTERFLY GROVE
25,000 monarch butterflies in one spot
Visit between late Oct - Feb, Free!

OSO FLACO LAKE
Boardwalk through arroyo willows
$5 parking - 1.5 miles round trip

GUADALUPE-NIPOMO DUNES
Remote dune trails - filming location of
Hidalgo, Pirates of the Caribbean

20) SAN LUIS OBISPO
1 hour 20 minutes Drive Time
72 miles

2 MILES

N

San Simeon
Cambria
Harmony
Cayucos
MORRO BAY
Morro Bay
Los Osos
MONTANA DE ORO
SAN LUIS OBISPO
Avila Beach
Pismo Beach
Grover Beach
Arroyo Grande
Oceano
Callender
Guadalupe
EMBARCADERO
MORRO BAY
MAIN
SPOONERS COVE
ISLAY
CORALLINA COVE
GROTTO ROCK
MONTANA DE ORO

SAN LUIS OBISPO

Best Coastal Secrets of San Luis Obispo: Local Advice from Laura Knudson

Morro Rock Natural Preserve is a picturesque place to stretch your legs while taking in the views of Morro Rock and the abundant local wildlife, including sea birds, seals, otters, and other marine life. It's especially beautiful at sunset where you can catch the sun disappearing behind Morro Rock from the adjacent sand dunes. Come prepared for chilly and strong winds even in the summer months.

Cayucos is a hidden gem along the PCH with the authentic small-town vibe of an original California beach town. You won't find any chain restaurants or big box stores, but you can reel in some of the best fish tacos along the coast at Ruddell's Smokehouse, rummage for second-hand vinyl records or antiques on Ocean Avenue, and savor the famous sea salt cookies at the Brown Butter Cookie Company.

Seaside Motel is a family owned and operated boutique hotel in the beach town of Cayucos. Just blocks from the ocean, the Seaside Motel feels like a true getaway with just a handful of rooms, each tailored to a unique theme and décor, and a relaxing garden that overlooks the water. Don't let their name fool you -- this place is one of the best-kept secrets along the California coast!

At the Piedras Blancas Elephant Seal Rookery, you'll see the wonderfully beautiful elephant seals, aptly named for their elephant-like noses (on the males) and their incredible size, as the second largest seal on the planet! Open 365 days a year, photo ops abound as visitors may see elephant seals breed, birth, or come ashore to molt. Be sure to visit the Friends of the Elephant Seals office located south of the rookery site in San Simeon for a free orientation to inform your visit.

Laura Knudson is a content creator and storyteller based in San Diego, CA. She is Director of Marketing for GLP Films, a film production and marketing agency dedicated to authentic storytelling for the travel industry. Say hello at @lauramknudson.

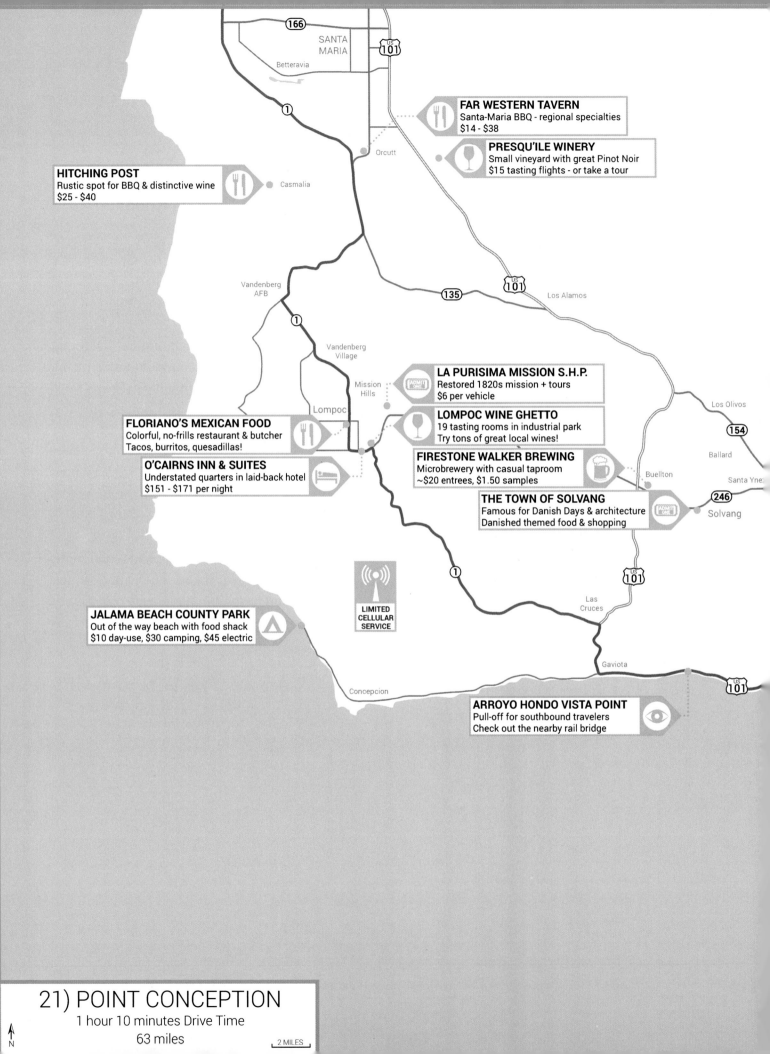

FAR WESTERN TAVERN
Santa-Maria BBQ - regional specialties
$14 - $38

PRESQU'ILE WINERY
Small vineyard with great Pinot Noir
$15 tasting flights - or take a tour

HITCHING POST
Rustic spot for BBQ & distinctive wine
$25 - $40

LA PURISIMA MISSION S.H.P.
Restored 1820s mission + tours
$6 per vehicle

FLORIANO'S MEXICAN FOOD
Colorful, no-frills restaurant & butcher
Tacos, burritos, quesadillas!

LOMPOC WINE GHETTO
19 tasting rooms in industrial park
Try tons of great local wines!

O'CAIRNS INN & SUITES
Understated quarters in laid-back hotel
$151 - $171 per night

FIRESTONE WALKER BREWING
Microbrewery with casual taproom
~$20 entrees, $1.50 samples

THE TOWN OF SOLVANG
Famous for Danish Days & architecture
Danished themed food & shopping

LIMITED
CELLULAR
SERVICE

JALAMA BEACH COUNTY PARK
Out of the way beach with food shack
$10 day-use, $30 camping, $45 electric

ARROYO HONDO VISTA POINT
Pull-off for southbound travelers
Check out the nearby rail bridge

21) POINT CONCEPTION
1 hour 10 minutes Drive Time
63 miles

2 MILES

N

POINT CONCEPTION

Santa Barbara Channel

The pacific coast runs almost perfectly north-south for over 1000 mile from Neah Bay on the Olympic Peninsula all the way down to Point Conception in California. The Santa Barbara Channel, a 70 mile long 24 mile wide body of water, is the first major change in this orientation. The Pacific Coast Highway runs along the northern edge of the channel past Santa Barbara and into Ventura. To the south you'll find the five islands that make up Channel Islands National Park, reachable only by ferry or personal boat.

The middle of the channel is a major shipping route for Los Angeles and Long Beach. It is also home to a number of deepwater oil fields, most infamously the Dos Cuadras Offshore field. In 1969, just one year after oil was discovered here, there was a major spill resulting in over 100,000 barrels of crude oil being released into the water. At the time this was the largest oil spill in American history. Now it ranks as the third largest after Deepwater Horizon and Exxon Valdez. One outcome of this massive spill was the creating of new environmental legislation and the founding of Earth Day.

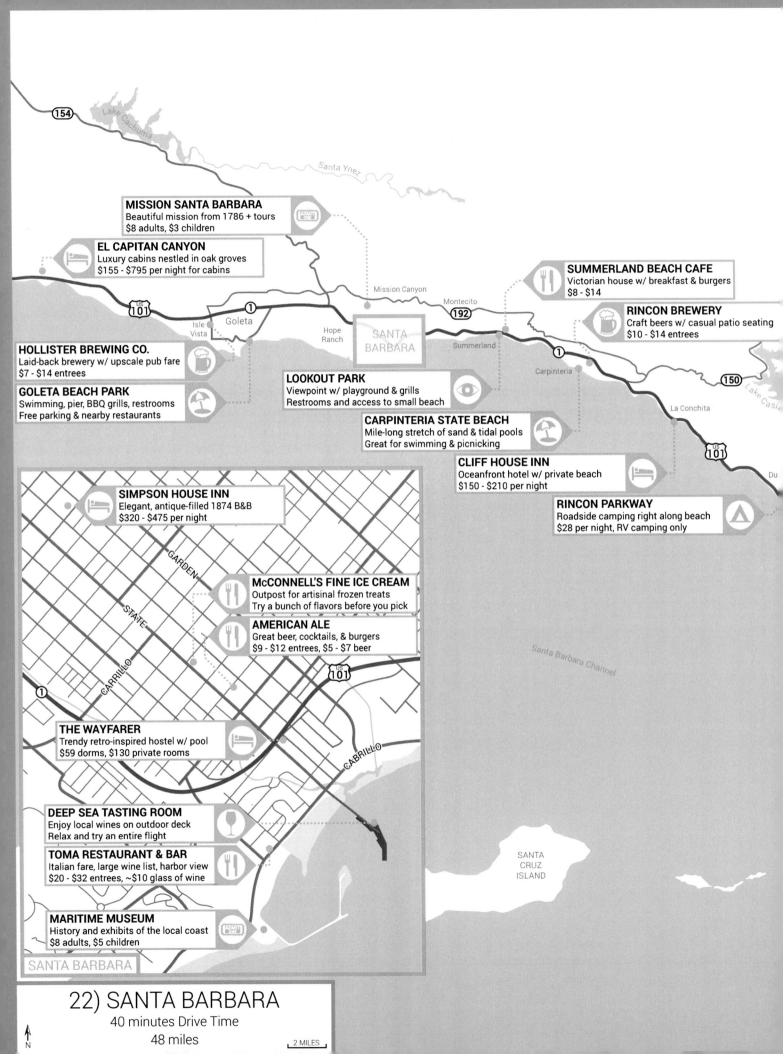

MISSION SANTA BARBARA
Beautiful mission from 1786 + tours
$8 adults, $3 children

EL CAPITAN CANYON
Luxury cabins nestled in oak groves
$155 - $795 per night for cabins

SUMMERLAND BEACH CAFE
Victorian house w/ breakfast & burgers
$8 - $14

RINCON BREWERY
Craft beers w/ casual patio seating
$10 - $14 entrees

HOLLISTER BREWING CO.
Laid-back brewery w/ upscale pub fare
$7 - $14 entrees

GOLETA BEACH PARK
Swimming, pier, BBQ grills, restrooms
Free parking & nearby restaurants

LOOKOUT PARK
Viewpoint w/ playground & grills
Restrooms and access to small beach

CARPINTERIA STATE BEACH
Mile-long stretch of sand & tidal pools
Great for swimming & picnicking

CLIFF HOUSE INN
Oceanfront hotel w/ private beach
$150 - $210 per night

SIMPSON HOUSE INN
Elegant, antique-filled 1874 B&B
$320 - $475 per night

RINCON PARKWAY
Roadside camping right along beach
$28 per night, RV camping only

McCONNELL'S FINE ICE CREAM
Outpost for artisinal frozen treats
Try a bunch of flavors before you pick

AMERICAN ALE
Great beer, cocktails, & burgers
$9 - $12 entrees, $5 - $7 beer

THE WAYFARER
Trendy retro-inspired hostel w/ pool
$59 dorms, $130 private rooms

DEEP SEA TASTING ROOM
Enjoy local wines on outdoor deck
Relax and try an entire flight

TOMA RESTAURANT & BAR
Italian fare, large wine list, harbor view
$20 - $32 entrees, ~$10 glass of wine

MARITIME MUSEUM
History and exhibits of the local coast
$8 adults, $5 children

SANTA BARBARA

Santa Barbara Channel

SANTA CRUZ ISLAND

22) SANTA BARBARA
40 minutes Drive Time
48 miles

2 MILES

N

SOUTHERN CALIFORNIA

Santa Barbara marks the threshold to the southern California section of the pacific coast. From here on south, it's miles-upon-miles of beautiful sand beaches, palm-lined streets, and thriving coastal cities. The best way to enjoy southern California is by diving straight into the beachside culture. Here are some ways to do it:

*   Grab a surfboard (and perhaps take a few lessons) and drop into a wave at any of the countless famous surfing spots
*   Put on your fancy shoes as you shop (or just stroll) along the 3rd Street Promenade or Marine Avenue
*   Spend an entire day on one beach -- places like Venice, Huntington, and Santa Monica have every-thing you could possibly want

Of course, there are also some spectacular hikes (most notably along the Malibu coast and at Torrey Pines), interesting attractions (like the Getty Villa), and unique breweries (don't miss Stone Brewing!) to round everything out.

There is truly something for everyone here.

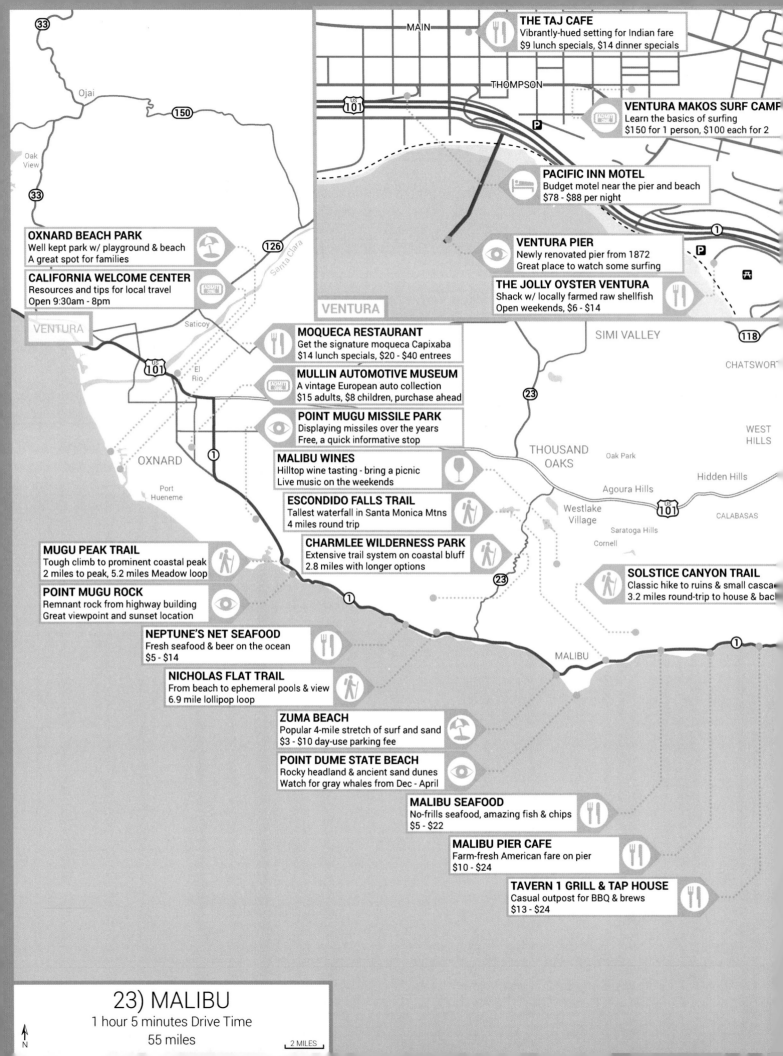

THE TAJ CAFE
Vibrantly-hued setting for Indian fare
$9 lunch specials, $14 dinner specials

MAIN

THOMPSON

VENTURA MAKOS SURF CAMP
Learn the basics of surfing
$150 for 1 person, $100 each for 2

PACIFIC INN MOTEL
Budget motel near the pier and beach
$78 - $88 per night

VENTURA PIER
Newly renovated pier from 1872
Great place to watch some surfing

THE JOLLY OYSTER VENTURA
Shack w/ locally farmed raw shellfish
Open weekends, $6 - $14

VENTURA

SIMI VALLEY

CHATSWOR

OXNARD BEACH PARK
Well kept park w/ playground & beach
A great spot for families

CALIFORNIA WELCOME CENTER
Resources and tips for local travel
Open 9:30am - 8pm

VENTURA

Saticoy

El Rio

MOQUECA RESTAURANT
Get the signature moqueca Capixaba
$14 lunch specials, $20 - $40 entrees

MULLIN AUTOMOTIVE MUSEUM
A vintage European auto collection
$15 adults, $8 children, purchase ahead

POINT MUGU MISSILE PARK
Displaying missiles over the years
Free, a quick informative stop

WEST
HILLS

THOUSAND
OAKS

Oak Park

MALIBU WINES
Hilltop wine tasting - bring a picnic
Live music on the weekends

Hidden Hills

Agoura Hills

OXNARD

Port
Hueneme

ESCONDIDO FALLS TRAIL
Tallest waterfall in Santa Monica Mtns
4 miles round trip

Westlake
Village

CALABASAS

Saratoga Hills

Cornell

MUGU PEAK TRAIL
Tough climb to prominent coastal peak
2 miles to peak, 5.2 miles Meadow loop

CHARMLEE WILDERNESS PARK
Extensive trail system on coastal bluff
2.8 miles with longer options

SOLSTICE CANYON TRAIL
Classic hike to ruins & small casca
3.2 miles round-trip to house & bac

POINT MUGU ROCK
Remnant rock from highway building
Great viewpoint and sunset location

NEPTUNE'S NET SEAFOOD
Fresh seafood & beer on the ocean
$5 - $14

MALIBU

NICHOLAS FLAT TRAIL
From beach to ephemeral pools & view
6.9 mile lollipop loop

ZUMA BEACH
Popular 4-mile stretch of surf and sand
$3 - $10 day-use parking fee

POINT DUME STATE BEACH
Rocky headland & ancient sand dunes
Watch for gray whales from Dec - April

MALIBU SEAFOOD
No-frills seafood, amazing fish & chips
$5 - $22

MALIBU PIER CAFE
Farm-fresh American fare on pier
$10 - $24

TAVERN 1 GRILL & TAP HOUSE
Casual outpost for BBQ & brews
$13 - $24

Ojai

Oak
View

Santa Clara

23) MALIBU
1 hour 5 minutes Drive Time
55 miles

2 MILES

N

MALIBU

5 Great Day Hikes just off the PCH: Local advice from Casey Schreiner

The Pacific Coast Highway hugs the seaside edge of the Santa Monica Mountains National Recreation Area – the country's largest urban unit of the National Park System. A patchwork of public and private lands provides unparalleled outdoor opportunities for Southern Californians.

Most of these trails stay cooler than their inland counterparts but summer and fall heat can be brutal. Hike early in the morning or in the evening, or wait for the winter and spring when they trails explode with native wildflowers.

Here are five great day hikes you can do without having to go too far off the PCH.

1) MUGU PEAK
A tough climb to a prominent coastal peak, with options to explore extensive meadows in Point Mugu State Park. (2 miles RT to peak. Meadow loop 5.2 miles)

2) NICHOLAS FLAT
A longer lollipop loop from the beach to a series of hidden meadows and ephemeral ponds overlooking the Ocean and Boney Mountain. (6.9 miles)

3) CHARMLEE WILDERNESS PARK
An extensive system of easy trails on a coastal bluff overlooking Malibu. Great views of the Channel Islands and an excellent nature center. (2.8 miles, length may vary)

4) ESCONDIDO FALLS
The tallest waterfall in the Santa Monica Mountains – with an easily accessible lower tier and a more challenging upper for experienced scramblers. (4 miles)

5) SOLSTICE CANYON
A classic SoCal hike to the ruins of a burned down mansion next to a trickling cascade. (3.2 miles to the house and back, with longer options)

Casey Schreiner is the founder and editor in chief of Modern Hiker, the number one hiking blog on the West Coast. Since 2006, Modern Hiker has provided hundreds of trail descriptions for hikes from Canada to Mexico and Colorado to Hawaii.

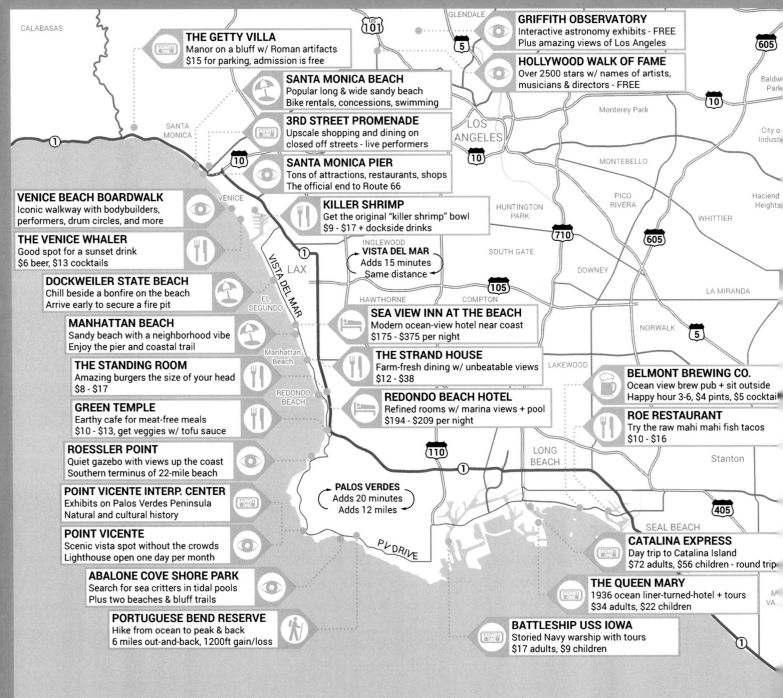

THE GETTY VILLA
Manor on a bluff w/ Roman artifacts
$15 for parking, admission is free

GRIFFITH OBSERVATORY
Interactive astronomy exhibits - FREE
Plus amazing views of Los Angeles

HOLLYWOOD WALK OF FAME
Over 2500 stars w/ names of artists,
musicians & directors - FREE

SANTA MONICA BEACH
Popular long & wide sandy beach
Bike rentals, concessions, swimming

3RD STREET PROMENADE
Upscale shopping and dining on
closed off streets - live performers

SANTA MONICA PIER
Tons of attractions, restaurants, shops
The official end to Route 66

VENICE BEACH BOARDWALK
Iconic walkway with bodybuilders,
performers, drum circles, and more

KILLER SHRIMP
Get the original "killer shrimp" bowl
$9 - $17 + dockside drinks

VISTA DEL MAR
Adds 15 minutes
Same distance

THE VENICE WHALER
Good spot for a sunset drink
$6 beer, $13 cocktails

DOCKWEILER STATE BEACH
Chill beside a bonfire on the beach
Arrive early to secure a fire pit

SEA VIEW INN AT THE BEACH
Modern ocean-view hotel near coast
$175 - $375 per night

MANHATTAN BEACH
Sandy beach with a neighborhood vibe
Enjoy the pier and coastal trail

THE STRAND HOUSE
Farm-fresh dining w/ unbeatable views
$12 - $38

THE STANDING ROOM
Amazing burgers the size of your head
$8 - $17

REDONDO BEACH HOTEL
Refined rooms w/ marina views + pool
$194 - $209 per night

BELMONT BREWING CO.
Ocean view brew pub + sit outside
Happy hour 3-6, $4 pints, $5 cocktail

GREEN TEMPLE
Earthy cafe for meat-free meals
$10 - $13, get veggies w/ tofu sauce

ROE RESTAURANT
Try the raw mahi mahi fish tacos
$10 - $16

ROESSLER POINT
Quiet gazebo with views up the coast
Southern terminus of 22-mile beach

POINT VICENTE INTERP. CENTER
Exhibits on Palos Verdes Peninsula
Natural and cultural history

PALOS VERDES
Adds 20 minutes
Adds 12 miles

POINT VICENTE
Scenic vista spot without the crowds
Lighthouse open one day per month

CATALINA EXPRESS
Day trip to Catalina Island
$72 adults, $56 children - round trip

ABALONE COVE SHORE PARK
Search for sea critters in tidal pools
Plus two beaches & bluff trails

THE QUEEN MARY
1936 ocean liner-turned-hotel + tours
$34 adults, $22 children

PORTUGUESE BEND RESERVE
Hike from ocean to peak & back
6 miles out-and-back, 1200ft gain/loss

BATTLESHIP USS IOWA
Storied Navy warship with tours
$17 adults, $9 children

24) LOS ANGELES
2 hour 5 minutes Drive Time
60 miles

2 MILES

N

LOS ANGELES

One Day along the Venice Beach Boardwalk: Local advice from Evan White

Start your morning with a cup of coffee, and a stroll down the Santa Monica Pier. You'll get a fresh perspective on the city, and an amazing view of the Santa Monica Mountains... As well as some great angles to snap pics of the surfers!

Next up, get your shopping fix on the 3rd Street Promenade, and Main Street. Both venues offer different shops and vibes, from a traditional mall in an outdoor setting to small boutiques and mom and pop shops on Main Street.

Heading south, check into your hotel along the World Famous Venice Boardwalk. We recommend either the Venice Beach Suites and Hotel, or Breeze Suites. Both offer amazing views of the ocean, and a rooftop deck for taking in the rays.

After check in, rent a Segway or tandem bicycle (don't forget your helmets) and head down the bike path just a short 3 miles to Marina Del Rey. On your way, stop off on Abbot Kinney for some window shopping in the coolest neighborhood in the US.

Just south of Santa Monica & Venice Beach is another LA gem, Marina Del Rey! Get yourself over to Fisherman's Village for amazing views of the many sail and motor boats that fill this area. Then, push your ticket for a fun filled ride 75 feet in the air under a parasail!

This trip up the beach (over the water) will take you north back to the Santa Monica Pier, and then back to Marina Del Rey... just in time for a sunset drink at the Venice Whaler! With views of the Venice Pier, and a stellar dinner and drink selection, you'll be good to go!

A short walk back to the hotel of your choice, then before you leave town don't miss a bloody marry at the Terrace Restaurant with perfect view of the beach and early morning surf clubs!

Enjoy your trip!

Evan White, CEO of the Venice Boardwalk App where you can find all of the amazing offerings from Marina Del Rey to Santa Monica. From local murals, bars, restaurants, famous attractions, and more.

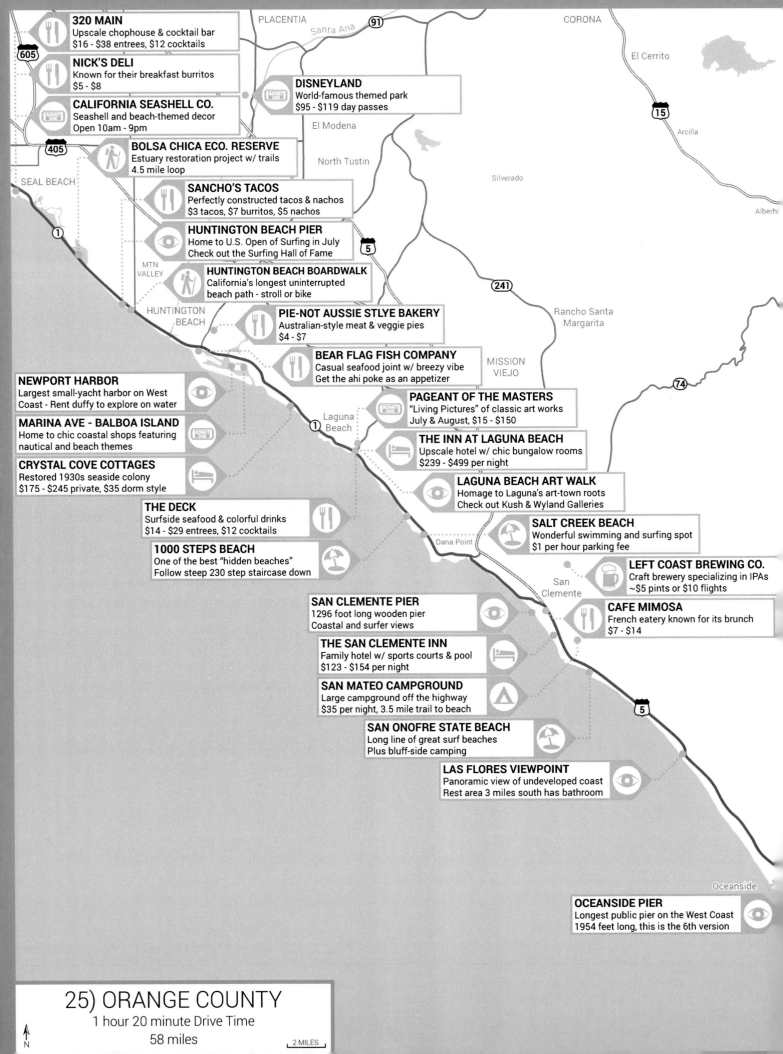

320 MAIN
Upscale chophouse & cocktail bar
$16 - $38 entrees, $12 cocktails

NICK'S DELI
Known for their breakfast burritos
$5 - $8

CALIFORNIA SEASHELL CO.
Seashell and beach-themed decor
Open 10am - 9pm

DISNEYLAND
World-famous themed park
$95 - $119 day passes

BOLSA CHICA ECO. RESERVE
Estuary restoration project w/ trails
4.5 mile loop

SANCHO'S TACOS
Perfectly constructed tacos & nachos
$3 tacos, $7 burritos, $5 nachos

HUNTINGTON BEACH PIER
Home to U.S. Open of Surfing in July
Check out the Surfing Hall of Fame

HUNTINGTON BEACH BOARDWALK
California's longest uninterrupted
beach path - stroll or bike

PIE-NOT AUSSIE STLYE BAKERY
Australian-style meat & veggie pies
$4 - $7

BEAR FLAG FISH COMPANY
Casual seafood joint w/ breezy vibe
Get the ahi poke as an appetizer

NEWPORT HARBOR
Largest small-yacht harbor on West
Coast - Rent duffy to explore on water

MARINA AVE - BALBOA ISLAND
Home to chic coastal shops featuring
nautical and beach themes

CRYSTAL COVE COTTAGES
Restored 1930s seaside colony
$175 - $245 private, $35 dorm style

PAGEANT OF THE MASTERS
"Living Pictures" of classic art works
July & August, $15 - $150

THE INN AT LAGUNA BEACH
Upscale hotel w/ chic bungalow rooms
$239 - $499 per night

LAGUNA BEACH ART WALK
Homage to Laguna's art-town roots
Check out Kush & Wyland Galleries

THE DECK
Surfside seafood & colorful drinks
$14 - $29 entrees, $12 cocktails

1000 STEPS BEACH
One of the best "hidden beaches"
Follow steep 230 step staircase down

SALT CREEK BEACH
Wonderful swimming and surfing spot
$1 per hour parking fee

LEFT COAST BREWING CO.
Craft brewery specializing in IPAs
~$5 pints or $10 flights

SAN CLEMENTE PIER
1296 foot long wooden pier
Coastal and surfer views

CAFE MIMOSA
French eatery known for its brunch
$7 - $14

THE SAN CLEMENTE INN
Family hotel w/ sports courts & pool
$123 - $154 per night

SAN MATEO CAMPGROUND
Large campground off the highway
$35 per night, 3.5 mile trail to beach

SAN ONOFRE STATE BEACH
Long line of great surf beaches
Plus bluff-side camping

LAS FLORES VIEWPOINT
Panoramic view of undeveloped coast
Rest area 3 miles south has bathroom

OCEANSIDE PIER
Longest public pier on the West Coast
1954 feet long, this is the 6th version

25) ORANGE COUNTY
1 hour 20 minute Drive Time
58 miles

2 MILES

ORANGE COUNTY

Orange County Beaches: Which one to Visit? Local advice from Pepe Avila

Each Orange County coastal community has their own very distinct personality, landscape, flavor, and offerings. If you only had to visit one, here's how I would describe each city in one word to let you decide the best destination for yourself: Seal Beach: **charming**; Huntington Beach: **laid-back**; Newport Beach: **sophisticated**; Laguna Beach: **eclectic**.

SEAL BEACH
Driving on PCH from one end of Seal Beach to the other takes just three-minutes, passing through three stoplights. Seal Beach is everything you want a SoCal surf community to be - casual and sleepy with plenty of sand and surf. Beach cruisers and drying wetsuits are outside almost all the beach bungalows and charming Main St. has mature trees lining the sidewalks giving ample shade to stroll leisurely into one mom and pop shop, café and local business after the next.

HUNTINGTON BEACH
The go-to destination for surf lifestyle, Huntington Beach has 10 miles of uninterrupted coastline with plenty of spots to surf or just watch the pros. With the most consistent waves on the West Coast and surfing as a way of life, this is the only place that can be called Surf City USA.

NEWPORT BEACH
Newport Beach is where sophistication, luxury and SoCal beach lifestyle all meet to form one idyllic seaside city. Newport Beach is widely celebrated for its vibrant yachting community alongside stylish accommodations, coastal cuisine, and upscale shopping. PCH travels straight through the heart of Newport Beach, but if you blink you could miss some of the area's most popular and pristine beaches. Balboa Peninsula and Corona del Mar beaches are accessed by traveling a very short distance off PCH.

LAGUNA BEACH
Laguna Beach was established as an artists' colony in the early 1900's, and much of its artistic past has remained in the present. There are more than 75 art galleries today and is home to many celebrated art festivals. In addition to its art scene, this bohemian-meets-affluent city also has more beachfront hotels than any other city in California and 20,000 acres of wilderness perfect for hiking and biking. Quaint, walkable downtown pours right into more than 30 scalloped beach coves along PCH, all with public access.

Pepe Avila is Visit Anaheim's Tourism Director, promoting tourism to Anaheim, Garden Grove and the greater Orange County.

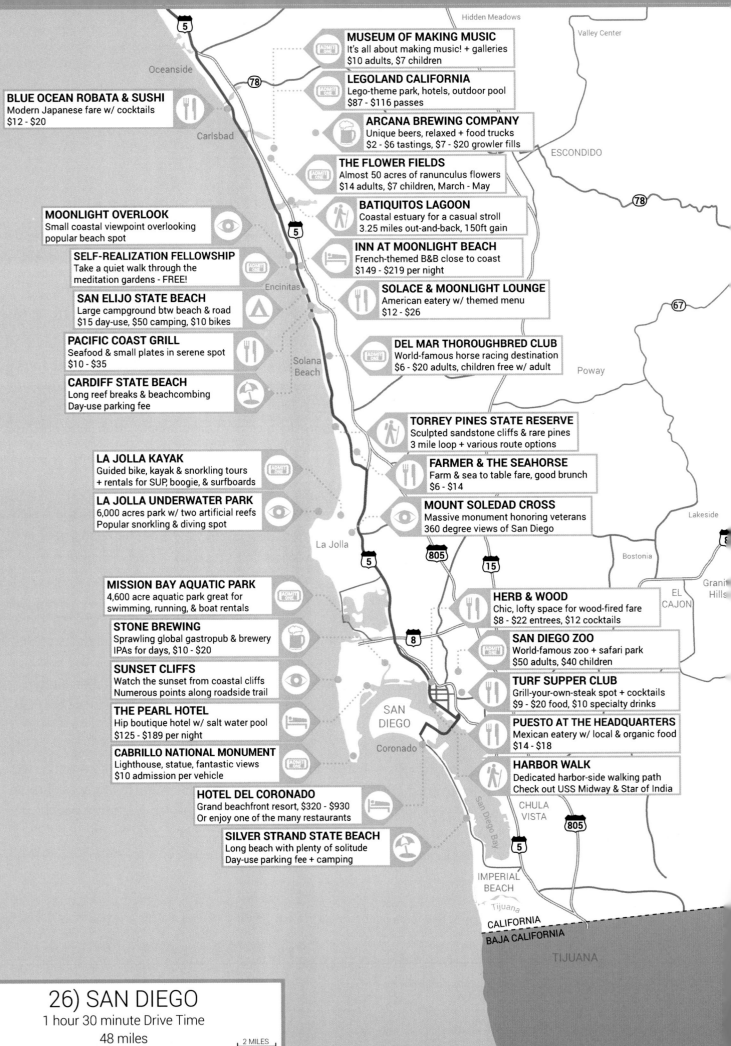

MUSEUM OF MAKING MUSIC
It's all about making music! + galleries
$10 adults, $7 children

LEGOLAND CALIFORNIA
Lego-theme park, hotels, outdoor pool
$87 - $116 passes

BLUE OCEAN ROBATA & SUSHI
Modern Japanese fare w/ cocktails
$12 - $20

ARCANA BREWING COMPANY
Unique beers, relaxed + food trucks
$2 - $6 tastings, $7 - $20 growler fills

THE FLOWER FIELDS
Almost 50 acres of ranunculus flowers
$14 adults, $7 children, March - May

MOONLIGHT OVERLOOK
Small coastal viewpoint overlooking
popular beach spot

BATIQUITOS LAGOON
Coastal estuary for a casual stroll
3.25 miles out-and-back, 150ft gain

SELF-REALIZATION FELLOWSHIP
Take a quiet walk through the
meditation gardens - FREE!

INN AT MOONLIGHT BEACH
French-themed B&B close to coast
$149 - $219 per night

SAN ELIJO STATE BEACH
Large campground btw beach & road
$15 day-use, $50 camping, $10 bikes

SOLACE & MOONLIGHT LOUNGE
American eatery w/ themed menu
$12 - $26

PACIFIC COAST GRILL
Seafood & small plates in serene spot
$10 - $35

DEL MAR THOROUGHBRED CLUB
World-famous horse racing destination
$6 - $20 adults, children free w/ adult

CARDIFF STATE BEACH
Long reef breaks & beachcombing
Day-use parking fee

TORREY PINES STATE RESERVE
Sculpted sandstone cliffs & rare pines
3 mile loop + various route options

LA JOLLA KAYAK
Guided bike, kayak & snorkling tours
+ rentals for SUP, boogie, & surfboards

FARMER & THE SEAHORSE
Farm & sea to table fare, good brunch
$6 - $14

LA JOLLA UNDERWATER PARK
6,000 acres park w/ two artificial reefs
Popular snorkling & diving spot

MOUNT SOLEDAD CROSS
Massive monument honoring veterans
360 degree views of San Diego

MISSION BAY AQUATIC PARK
4,600 acre aquatic park great for
swimming, running, & boat rentals

HERB & WOOD
Chic, lofty space for wood-fired fare
$8 - $22 entrees, $12 cocktails

STONE BREWING
Sprawling global gastropub & brewery
IPAs for days, $10 - $20

SAN DIEGO ZOO
World-famous zoo + safari park
$50 adults, $40 children

SUNSET CLIFFS
Watch the sunset from coastal cliffs
Numerous points along roadside trail

TURF SUPPER CLUB
Grill-your-own-steak spot + cocktails
$9 - $20 food, $10 specialty drinks

THE PEARL HOTEL
Hip boutique hotel w/ salt water pool
$125 - $189 per night

PUESTO AT THE HEADQUARTERS
Mexican eatery w/ local & organic food
$14 - $18

CABRILLO NATIONAL MONUMENT
Lighthouse, statue, fantastic views
$10 admission per vehicle

HARBOR WALK
Dedicated harbor-side walking path
Check out USS Midway & Star of India

HOTEL DEL CORONADO
Grand beachfront resort, $320 - $930
Or enjoy one of the many restaurants

SILVER STRAND STATE BEACH
Long beach with plenty of solitude
Day-use parking fee + camping

26) SAN DIEGO
1 hour 30 minute Drive Time
48 miles

2 MILES

N

SAN DIEGO

Spanish Missions in California

Between the years of 1769 and 1833, Catholic priests of the Franciscan order established 21 missions along the California coast from San Diego to Sonoma. These sites were a northern extension of the already established missions located in Baja California. Spain's purpose in creating the mission system was manyfold, including:

- To create a literate colony for New World expansion
- To make tax-paying citizens out of their conquered civilizations
- To assimilate indigenous populations into European culture and Catholic religion

San Diego and Monterey were the first missions established. From there, a mission site was designated according to the distance someone could ride in one day via horseback (about 30 miles). The road that linked the missions was called El Camino Real ("The Royal Highway"). Today, Highway 101 follows a significant portion of El Camino Real. In 1892, a series of 450 bells were placed along Highway 101 as road markers. This tradition of bell markers is still used today.

From 1769 to 1823, the mission system slowly worked on converting native people. Once baptized, they were forced to work and live on the mission. Over the 50 year mission period, an estimated 53,000 natives were converted and 15,000 died from disease. The missions never succeeded at become entirely self-sufficient, so they relied on continued financial support from Spain. When Mexico became an independent nation in 1821, the financial supply was cut off and many missions fell into disrepair and abandonment.

When California because a part of the United States in 1850, the missions were officially disbanded. The native tribes were stripped of their lands and most were moved into designated reservations.

These California missions are the furthest northern expansion of Spanish colonization. The original plan was to continue their progress further north and more inland, but due to funding and other foreign affairs, this plan was never realized.

The surviving missions are the oldest buildings in California, offering insight into the history of Spain's colonization more than 300 years ago.

WASHINGTON - SAMPLE ITINERARY

- Start off your day with a Belgian waffle from Medina Cafe, then head over to the Seawall for a morning walk or bike ride.
- For lunch, enjoy locally-sourced ingredients at Forage.
- Either check out the market and shops at Granville Island, or visit the Museum of Anthropology in the afternoon.
- Start driving south, stopping at Flying Beaver Bar & Grill or Taverna Gorgona for dinner.
- Spend the night at either Birch Bay State Park or Fairhaven Village Inn.

DAY 2

- Continue south to the Orcas Island ferry in Anacortes, stopping for freshly baked bread at Breadfarm.
- Take the ferry over to Orcas Island.
- Spend you day scoping out local pottery, watching orca whales, hiking, and enjoying the views from Mount Constitution.
- Grab some shuck-your-own-oysters from Buck Bay Shellfish Farms.
- Spend the night at either Moran State Park or Pebble Cove Farm.

DAY 3

- Jump on the morning ferry back to Anacortes.
- Grab brunch from Gere-A-Deli and head south to Deception Pass State Park. Make sure to stop at Rosario Head for beautiful coastal views and the Outdoor Blueprint logo tree (tag #OutsideYourself to share!).
- Spend the afternoon at Deception Pass beach - check out the bridge from above and below.
- Drive to Keystone for a ferry ride over to Port Townsend. Grab some fish & chips from Keystone Cafe while you wait.
- If it's low tide, head out for an evening hike along the Dungeness Spit.
- Spend the night at either Sequim Bay State Park or Green House Inn on the Bay.

DAY 4

- Grab breakfast at First Street Haven before driving up to the Hurricane Ridge Visitors Center.
- Hike up Hurricane Hill, then cruise back down to town for lunch.
- Choose to explore either the Washington Lavender Farm, hike to Olympic Hot Springs, or relax at Harbinger Winery in the afternoon.

- Eat dinner at Next Door Gastropub and enjoy the evening in Port Angeles.
- Stay at the Olympic Lodge or Heart O'The Hills Campground for the night.

DAY 5

- Head west on Highway 101, stopping at Marymere Falls and the La Poel picnic area along the way.
- Drive up to Sol Duc for the hike and/or a soak in the resort hot springs.
- Continue to the town of Forks, where the popular book/film franchise Twilight was based.
- Choose to explore the tidepools and sea stacks of Rialto Beach or the sand expanse of Second Beach.
- Stay at either the Quillayute River Resort or Mora Campground for the night.

DAY 6

- Drive into the Hoh valley.
- Take a peek inside the visitors center before hiking one of the area's trails.
- Choose to either stop at the Big Cedar and Big Spruce at Lake Quinault or enjoy the quirky museums and history of Aberdeen.
- Stop at Westport Winery for a relaxing evening tasting.
- Take the Westport option and stay at either Westport Marina Cottages or Grayland Beach State Park.

DAY 7

- Take a sunrise hike along Westport's Light Trail.
- Visit Grays Harbor Lighthouse and the Maritime Museum.
- Head south on Highway 105, stopping to enjoy the beach at Grayland Beach State Park.
- Grab lunch at Pitchwood Alehouse and stop at the Northwest Carriage Museum if you're interested.
- Take a short walk along the Willapa National Wildlife Refuge Salmon Trail before continuing into Seaview.
- Explore the Discovery Trail, Cape Disappointment State Park, and various eateries found in town.
- Stay at the Shelburne Inn for a classic bed & breakfast, the Sou'wester Lodge for quirky trailers and suites, or Cape Disappointment State Park for camping.
- Continue your journey south into Oregon across the Astoria-Megler Bridge or circle back north via Oregon Highway 30 to Interstate 5.

OREGON - SAMPLE ITINERARY

DAY 1

- Spend the morning exploring the marina and shops along the Riverwalk in Astoria, give yourself plenty of time to check out the Columbia River Maritime Museum.
- Stop at Buoy Beer Company for lunch and an afternoon brew then head to the Astoria Column for a relaxing walk and excellent views.
- Grab dinner at Northwest Wild and stay at either the Norblad Hotel or camp in nearby Fort Stevens State Park.

DAY 2

- Head out to the beach at sunrise and grab some pictures of the Peter Iredale shipwreck.
- Continue south and stop at either the Seaside Turnaround to check out the shops or hike at Ecola State Park.
- Pull over at Neahkahnie Viewpoint (highest along the Oregon coast) on the way to the Tillamook Cheese Factory (free samples!).
- Grab lunch at Blue Heron Cheese Company then jump on the Three Capes Scenic Route.
- Check out the lighthouse and Octopus Tree at Cape Meares and stop at Lex's Cool Stuff for brownies and 2nd hand shopping.
- Hike the 4.8 mile Cape Trail then head into Pacific City for dinner at the Pelican Pub.
- Stay at Pacific City or camp to the north at Cape Lookout.

DAY 3

- Grab breakfast at Cafe on Hawk Creek on the way down to Jennifer Sears Glass Art Studio.
- Check out glass art being made or maybe make your own, then continue south to watch for ocean birds at Boiler Bay Scenic Viewpoint.
- Head out on a whale watching tour out of Depoe Bay. Afterwards taste some salt water taffy at Ainslee's and get lunch at Gracie's Sea Hag.
- As you continue south turn off onto Otter Crest Scenic Loop where you can taste some wine while watching surf crash at the Devil's Punchbowl.
- Tour Yaquina Lighthouse or spend some time walking the beach at South Beach State Park.
- Enjoy a hot bowl of slumgullion at Luna Sea.
- Stay at the Fireside Motel or camp at Cape Perpetua State Park.

DAY 4

- Take a morning stroll down the Hobbit Trail to the beach, then stop at the Sea Lion Caves on your way to Florence.
- Spend the late morning exploring the sand dunes either by renting an ATV or taking a hike.
- Grab lunch at Harbor Light Restaurant or the Fishermen's Seafood Market. In the afternoon take the Cape Arago scenic loop, stopping to enjoy the parks along the way.
- Explore the town of Bandon and eat dinner at the Bandon Fish Market.
- Stay at the Bandon Beach Motel or camp at Bullards Beach State Park.

DAY 5

- Spend the morning stopping at sights like Face Rock, Cape Blanco Lighthouse, and Battle Rock Park.
- Eat lunch at the Crazy Norwegian's Fish & Chips then hike up the Humbug Mountain Trail.
- Check in to the Gold Beach Inn then drive down to Myer's Creek Beach for the sunset.
- Enjoy dinner at the Barnacle Bistro.

DAY 6

- Continue your journey to California, stopping at the Natural Bridges Viewpoint on the way.

NORTHERN CA - SAMPLE ITINERARY

DAY 1

- Grab a photo at the Oregon and California state border, then pick up a pastry at Vita Cucina Bakery in Crescent City.
- Drive up Howland Hill Road, making sure to stop and hike through Stout Grove on your way.
- Hit Hiouchi Visitors Center for more information on the park before driving back to Crescent City for the night.
- Stay at Lighthouse Inn and grab a classy seafood dinner at Chart Room Restaurant.
- Watch the sunset over Battery Point Lighthouse, explore the island if the tides permit.

DAY 2

- Go for a quick morning hike on the Yurok Loop Trail, then catch a gondola ride through the forest at Trees of Mystery.
- Cruise down Newton B Drury scenic route before jutting off the main route to hike through Fern Canyon.
- Watch for elk as you dodge over to Lady Bird Johnson Grove, then grab a late lunch at Snack Shack.
- Hit other quick highlights such at the hike up Trinidad Head and the world's tallest totem pole before setting in for the night at the Redwood Lily Guest House.

DAY 3

- Get a massive breakfast at Samoa Cookhouse, then walk it off at Humboldt Bay National Wildlife Refuge.
- Stop by the Loleta Cheese Factory for some samples before checking out the Victorian buildings at Ferndale.
- Work your way down the Avenue of the Giants, making sure to stop at Founders Grove, Rockefeller Grove, and the Shrine Drive-Thru Tree.
- Grab a calzone and a brew on the patio of Avenue Cafe.
- Take a side trip down to Black Sands Beach.
- Stay at either the Benbow Historic Inn or Hidden Springs Campground.

DAY 4

- Meet back up with the ocean along your drive south - don't miss the Westport Whale.
- Hit the Laguna Point Boardwalk and Glass Beach in Fort Bragg, and stop at Egghead's Restaurant on the way out.
- Spend an hour or two relaxing at Jug Handle State Beach before touring Point Arena Light Station.
- Spend the evening in Mendocino eating at Cafe Beaujolais and walking along Point Mendocino.
- Head down to Manchester State Park or Wharf Master's Inn for the night.

DAY 5

- Grab some breakfast pastries at Franny's Cup and Saucer before exploring bowling ball rock formations at Schooner Gulch State Beach.
- Check out the Pygmy Forest at Salt Point State Park or overlook the ocean while sipping wine at Fort Ross Vineyard.
- Spend the afternoon exploring the Sonoma Coast beaches.
- Grab dinner at Terrapin Creek Cafe and stay overnight in Bodega Bay at either Bodega Dunes Campground or Bodega Harbor Inn.

DAY 6

- Swing by the Potter School House (one filming location for "The Birds") then get a locally sourced breakfast at Estero Cafe.
- Snap a picture of the Point Reyes Shipwreck and the Cypress Tree Tunnel on your way out to Chimney Rock Trail.
- Grab some Hog Island Oysters and spend your afternoon kayaking, horseback riding, or hiking.
- Finish up with a margarita on the beach before spending your final night at Steep Ravine Campground.

CA CENTRAL COAST - SAMPLE ITINERARY

DAY 1

- Stop at Muir Beach Overlook before driving over the Golden Gate Bridge into San Francisco.
- Head into Golden Gate Park and take the elevator to the De Young Museum viewing deck for a bird's eye view of the city.
- Grab a late breakfast at Devil's Teeth Baking Company, then check out Lands End and the Sutro Baths.
- Head south to Devil's Slide Trail and get a late lunch lobster roll sandwich at Sam's Chowder House and a beer at Hop Dogma Brewing Company.
- Explore Maverick's Beach, grab dinner at Via Uno Cucina, and spend the night at Point Montara Hostel.

DAY 2

- Wake up for an early morning stroll along the Half Moon Bay Coastal Trail, then grab a Bloody Mary at San Gregorio General Store.
- Take a tour of Harley Farms and try some of their amazing cheese.
- Grab lunch to-go from Norm's Market and enjoy it at the hidden Shark Fin Cove.
- Stop at Natural Bridges on your way into Santa Cruz.
- Walk along the Santa Cruz Boardwalk and pier, then hit the road south towards Monterey. Stop to pick up some cheap and fresh produce on the way.
- Grab dinner at the Monterey Fish House, stay the night at Lover's Point Inn, wander along the coastal trail and Cannery Row in the evening.

DAY 3

- Visit the Monterey Bay Aquarium - get there right when it opens.
- Spend the morning and afternoon at the aquarium, perhaps take a jellyfish tour...
- Drive along 17 Mile Drive, stopping for a iconic picture of the Lone Cypress.
- Grab dinner at Hula's Island Grill and spend another night in Monterey.

DAY 4

- Head out early for a trip to Point Lobos State Reserve.
- Wind your way down the Big Sur coastline. Don't miss Bixby Bridge, Pfeiffer Beach, McWay Falls, and Limekiln Falls as you go.
- Check out the Piedras Blancas Elephant Seal Rookery, then grab a burger at Sebastian's.
- Spend the night in Cambria at the Sand Pebbles Inn and Moonstone Beach.

DAY 5

- Have a relaxing morning before continuing south. Make sure to grab a salmon taco from Ruddell's on the way to Morro Bay.
- Rent some kayaks and explore the estuary and dunes.
- Stop at the Museum of Natural History before heading back into town for lunch at The Galley Seafood Grill.
- Drive down to Montana De Oro State Park and set up camp at environmental site #3.
- Hike along the Bluff Trail, exploring the tidal pools as you go.

DAY 6

- Continue south to Pismo Beach for a cinnamon roll breakfast.
- Spend the morning exploring the shopping and beach at Avila Beach followed by a relaxing soak at Sycamore Hot Spring Resort.
- Grab clam chowder in a bread bowl from Splash Cafe, then head to the Monarch Grove.
- Cruise down to Lompoc and visit the wine ghetto.
- Spend the night in Lompoc at O'Cairns Inn & Suites.

SOUTHERN CA - SAMPLE ITINERARY

DAY 1

- Take a morning tour of the Old Santa Barbara Mission, then choose your favorite ice cream flavor at McConnell's.
- Window shop along State Street on your way to lunch at American Ale.
- Head east to Carpinteria State Beach for some swimming.
- Grab dinner at The Taj Cafe in Ventura & watch the sunset from the pier.
- Camp along Rincon Parkway or stay at Pacific Inn Motel.

DAY 2

- Sign up with Ventura Makos Surf Camp for a morning lesson, followed by some oysters.
- Spend the afternoon touring the Mullin Automotive Museum or enjoying one of the many stunning hikes along the Malibu coastline.
- Grab an early dinner at Malibu Seafood (they have great fish & chips!).
- Drive north to Malibu Wines, grab a bottle, and enjoy the live music.
- Continue up to the Thousand Oaks area for some cheaper lodging options or head to Santa Monica to be right in the action.

DAY 3

- Check out the Getty Villa in the morning, followed by a swim at Santa Monica Beach.
- Enjoy all of the performers along the Venice Beach Boardwalk, then grab some food and drinks at The Venice Whaler.
- Spend the afternoon strolling along the 3rd Street Promenade.
- If you're in a meat mood, hit up The Standing Room for the biggest burger of your life, otherwise head to Green Temple for some amazing vegetarian fare.
- Stay at the Redondo Beach Hotel and enjoy an evening walk along the pier.

DAY 4

- Drive along the Palos Verdes Peninsula, stopping to enjoy the viewpoints and tidal pools along the way.
- Take a tour of either the Queen Mary or USS Iowa Battleship.
- Head over to Huntington Beach and grab lunch at Sancho's Tacos.
- Walk down the pier and watch the surfers at the home of the US Open of Surfing (don't miss the Hall of Fame!).
- Spend the afternoon strolling along the Huntington Beach Boardwalk, shopping along Marine Avenue on Balboa Island, or scoping out the art scene in Laguna Beach.
- Grab dinner at The Deck in Laguna Beach.
- Stay at either Crystal Cove Beach Cottages or The Inn at Laguna Beach.

DAY 5

- Head out for a morning walk along 1000 Steps Beach, then hit the road south.
- If it's spring, make sure to stop at the Field of Flowers.
- Grab brunch at the Farmer & the Seahorse, then take a walk along the sculpted sandstone cliffs of Torrey Pines State Natural Reserve.
- Check out the view from the Mount Soledad Cross.
- Jump in the water by way of snorkeling at the La Jolla Underwater Park or beaching and boating at Mission Bay.
- Head to Stone Brewing for delicious IPAs and sharables, then watch the sunset from the Silver Strand.
- Finish off with a stay at The Pearl Hotel.

ACKNOWLEDGEMENTS

I've driven almost every section of the pacific coast, but I can safely say that this road trip guide wouldn't be nearly the resource it is without the help of so many generous locals sharing their favorite spots.

Harrison Shotzbarger, Alex Bigus, Alexandra Talucci, Peter Keding, Ben Schwartz, Jennifer Bigus, Kevin O'Leary, Lindsay Babbitt, Zach Dahlmer, Kyle Johnson, Luke Goodman, Kim Olson, Tara Cappel, Daniel Howard, Katie Sherif, Madelyn Burkhart, Megan MacNee, Ashley Hamik, Kira Maixner, Mike Catania, Netanya Trimboli, James O'Hagan, Sriram Srinivasan, & Katrina Leo

Special thanks go out to the featured locals who let you in on their favorite spots.

Carol Zahorsky, Skyler Lanning, Jeremy Strober, Stephen Hoshaw, Aaron Altabet, Julie Murrell, Josh McNair, Dylan Gallagher, Casey Schreiner, Laura Knudson, Erin Ramsauer, Pepe Avila, Evan White, Robert Arends, & Sarah Weinberg

Finally, this guide probably wouldn't have been completed without the support of my wife, Sarah. Thanks for all of your help editing, marketing, and problem-solving. AND for making sure I kept eating while spending 12 hour days on this project. You're the best!

Made in the USA
Las Vegas, NV
17 June 2021